Snorkel Kaua'i

Guide to the Underwater World of Hawai'i • Judy and Mel Malinowski

Snorkel Kauai

Guide to the Underwater World of Hawaii

First Edition © 2001 by Judy and Mel Malinowski

Published by: Indigo Publications
                       920 Los Robles Avenue
                       Palo Alto, CA 94306 USA

                       SAN 298-9921
                       Publisher's symbol: Indigo CA

Printed in Hong Kong by C & C Offset Printing Co., Inc.

About the cover:

Camille Young painted this lovely saddleback butterflyfish in water-color especially for our cover. A graduate of the University of Hawai'i at O'ahu, she now lives in Moraga, California.

Dave Barry is renowned for his humorous essays and books. His love of the underwater world brings a special eloquence to these passages.

Quotes from "Blub Story", Tropic Magazine, © Dave Barry 1989.

Mahalo to the kind residents of Kaua'i for keeping the aloha tradition alive, Marta Jorasch, and many others.

Every effort has been made to provide accurate and reliable information and advice in this book. Venturing out into the ocean has inherent, ever-changing risks which must be evaluated in each situation by the persons involved. The authors and publishers are not responsible for any inconvenience, loss or injury sustained by our readers during their travels. Travel, swim and snorkel safely. When in doubt, err on the side of caution.

ISBN 0-9646680-4-1
Library of Congress Catalog Card Number: 00-111711

Contents

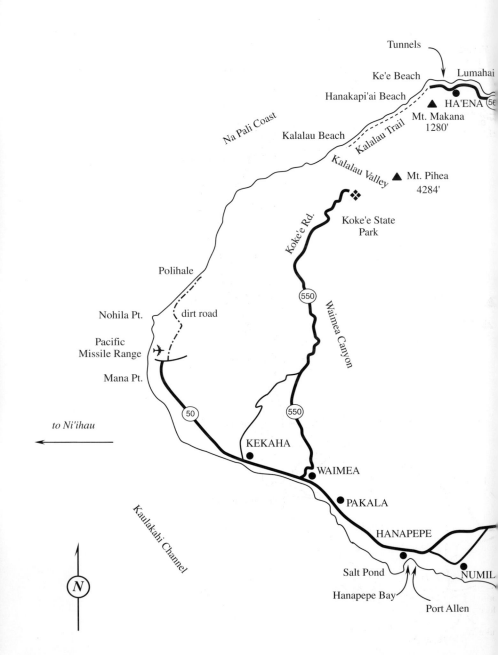

Tunnels

Ke'e Beach — Lumahai

Hanakapi'ai Beach — ▲ HA'ENA — 56

Na Pali Coast

Mt. Makana 1280'

Kalalau Beach

Kalalau Trail

Kalalau Valley — ▲ Mt. Pihea 4284'

Koke'e Rd.

Koke'e State Park

Polihale

550

Waimea Canyon

Nohila Pt. — dirt road

Pacific Missile Range

Mana Pt.

50

550

to Ni'ihau

KEKAHA

WAIMEA

PAKALA

HANAPEPE

Kaulakahi Channel

Salt Pond

NUMIL

Hanapepe Bay

Port Allen

N

4

Kaua'i Road Map

(Also see Snorkeling Site
Index Map on page 38)

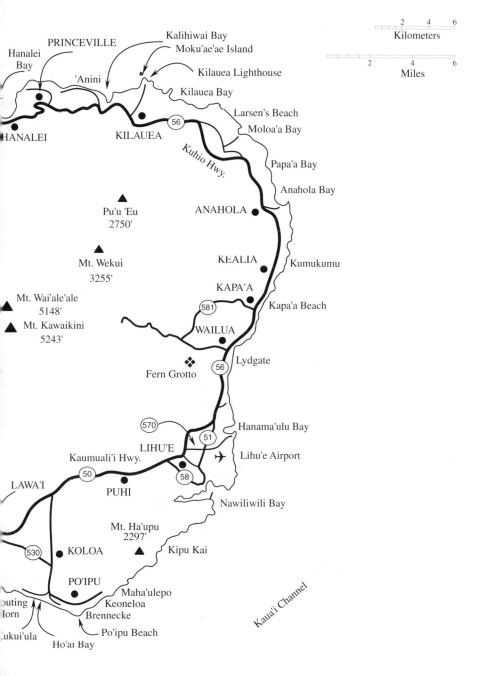

5

Dedicated to our public libraries and their role in the lifelong education of us all. Special thanks to the Hawai'i State Library System, which has contributed so much to our understanding of the natural world of Hawai'i.

Why Snorkel Kaua'i?

Kaua'i, the Garden Isle, offers lush, spectacular scenery straight out of your wildest tropical dreams. The oldest of the main Hawai'ian islands, Kaua'i is dramatically mountainous and nearly surrounded by fringing reefs, with numerous pristine beaches. Most of the coast can be reached by car, while the Na Pali Coast, Ni'ihau and Lehua Islands are just a boat excursion away.

Choose a snorkeling site by location, from gorgeous Ke'e, at the end of the road in the north, to secluded Maha'ulepo in the south, or child-safe Salt Pond in the west. Beginners will find Lydgate Park's protected pond satisfying, while advanced snorkelers can roam the extensive nearby reefs when weather permits.

With few sites fully protected inside a bay, everyone needs good advice to snorkel safely in Kaua'i. Seasons, swells, rain and tide level must all be considered, so it's best to have plenty of choices of where to go on a particular day. Few of Kaua'i's sites are well-marked, and some are very difficult to find without detailed maps.

Snorkel Kaua'i makes it easy

An active vacation is memorable for adventure as well as relaxation. Hassles and missteps finding out where to go can raise your blood pressure and waste your time. We've done extensive research that will help you quickly locate appropriate sites that fit your interests and abilities, saving your valuable vacation hours.

Snorkeling sites in Hawai'i are sometimes tricky because of changeable waves and currents, so it's best to get good advice before heading out. Everyone has had their share of unpleasant experiences due to vague directions as well as outdated or inaccurate information. We have created the Snorkel Hawai'i series as that savvy snorkeling buddy everyone needs. We've included many personal stories; see About the Authors on page 192 if you want to know a little more about us.

We have snorkeled all the major sites listed, and many that are not well known. The challenge lies in finding them quickly, as well as how to enter and exit, and where to snorkel, so you'll have a safe and rewarding experience. Our detailed maps and instructions will ease the uncertainty, saving you time and effort.

Try to visit Kaua'i at least once in your life and by all means don't miss the underwater world. Aloha!

– Judy and Mel Malinowski

Snorkeling is...

- easy
- relaxing
- fun
- floating on the surface of the sea
- breathing without effort through a tube
- peering into the water world through a mask
- open to any age, size, shape or ability

Who was the first snorkeler? As the fossil records include few petrified snorkels, we are free to speculate.

Among larger creatures, elephants are the pioneers and current champions, as they have known how to snorkel for countless generations. Once in a blue moon, you may see a elephant herd heading out to do lunch on an island off the coast of Tanzania, paddling along with their trunks held high. No one knows whether the hefty pachyderms enjoy the fish-watching, but you can bet a big liquid chuckle reverberates through the ranks of reef fish in the vicinity as the parade goes by.

As evolution continued, perhaps a clever member of the promising homo sapiens species saved his furry brow by hiding underwater from pursuers, breathing through a hollow reed. Masks came much later, so the fish probably looked a little fuzzy. Surviving to propagate his brainy kind, he founded a dynasty of snorkelers. Perhaps he actually liked the peaceful atmosphere down there, and a new sport was born.

Some of our readers may grumble that snorkeling is not a real sport: no rules, no score, no competition, scarcely aerobic, with hardly any equipment or clothing. We say to them: lighten up, you're on vacation!! Go for a long run later.

Incorrigible competitors can create their own competition by counting how many species they've seen or trying to spot the biggest or the most seen in one day. Everybody else can relax and just have fun being a part of nature's colorful, salty, wet, ancient home.

Basics

To snorkel you need only two things:

Snorkel
Saves lifting your head once a minute, wasting energy and disturbing the fish.

Mask
While you can see (poorly) without one, it keeps the water out of your eyes and lets you see clearly.

Rent them inexpensively at many local shops or buy them if you prefer. It's all the back-to-basics folks need to snorkel in calm warm water, where there aren't any currents or hazards.

Savvy snorkelers often add a few items to the list, based on years of experience, such as:

Swimsuit
Required by law in many localities. Added benefit: can save you from an occasional all-body sunburn.

Fins
Good if you want to swim with ease and speed like a fish. Saves energy. A must in Hawai'i, due to occasional strong currents. They protect your tender feet too.

T-shirt
Simple way to avoid or minimize sunburn on your back. Available everywhere.

Sunscreen
To slather on the tender exposed backside skin of your legs, neck, and the backs of your arms. Not optional in Hawai'i for light-skinned snorkelers.

Lycra Skin
A great all-body coverup for warm weather. Provides much better protection than a T-shirt, and saves gallons of sunscreen.

Wetsuit
For some, the Hawai'ian waters seem a bit chilly – not exactly pool-warm. Wetsuits range from simple T-shirt-like tops to full suits. Worth considering. Fringe benefit: free sun protection!

You're almost ready to get wet. But wait! You want to know even more technical detail? Every sport has an equipment list – it's what keeps sporting goods stores in business and your garage shelves full.

Gear Selection

Good snorkeling gear enables you to pay attention to the fish instead of uncomfortable distractions. Poor equipment will make you suffer in little ways, from pressure headaches caused by a too-tight mask, to blisters on your feet from ill-fitting fins. Consider your alternatives carefully before buying and you'll have more fun later.

Snorkel

Snorkels can be quite cheap. Be prepared to pony up $15 or more if you want them to last awhile and be comfortable. You'll appreciate a comfortable mouthpiece if you plan to snorkel for long. Watch out for hard edges – a good mouthpiece is smooth and chewy-soft.

Several new high tech models have been designed to minimize water coming down the tube from chop or an occasional swell overtopping you. We looked at these with mild skepticism until a choppy snorkeling trip had us coughing and clearing our snorkels every third breath. With our new snorkels, that water is diverted out before it makes it to the mouthpiece.

We tested a new snorkel by pouring buckets of water down the tube. The snorkeler didn't even notice! Our verdict is: the new technology works as advertised. Avoid the old "float ball at the top" versions.

We use the US Divers Impulse snorkel (about $35), but others may be equally effective. A friend recommends a Dacor model with corrugated, flexible neck. A bottom purge valve makes blowing out water smooth and easy, on those occasional cases when it is required. These nifty snorkels are well worth the higher price if you snorkel in choppy water or like to surface dive.

Snorkel Holder

This little guy holds your snorkel to your mask strap, so you don't keep dipping it in the sea. The standard is a simple figure 8 double loop that pulls over the snorkel tube, wraps around your mask strap, and then back over the tube. A hefty rubber band will work passably in a pinch.

The higher end snorkels often have a slot that allows the snorkel to be adjusted easily. It slides rather than having to be tugged. The standard Scuba snorkel position is on your left side. You might as well get used to it there since you may dive eventually.

Mask

Nothing can color your snorkeling experience more than an ill-fitting mask. Unless, of course, you get that all-body sunburn mentioned earlier. Don't settle for painful or leaky masks! If it hurts, it's not your problem – it's the mask that's wrong for you. In this case "pain, no gain" applies.

Simple variety store masks can cost as little as $10. Top-quality masks from a dive shop run upwards of $60. Consider starting out with a rental mask, paying a bit extra for the better quality models. As you gain more experience, you'll be in a better position to evaluate a mask before you lock yourself into one style.

You need a good fit to your particular facial geometry. Shops often tell you to place the mask on your face (without the strap) and breathe in. If the mask will stay in place, then they say you have found a good fit. However, nearly all masks will stay on my face under this test, yet some leak later!

Look for soft edges and a mask that conforms to your face even before drawing in your breath. There's a great deal of variance in where a mask rests on your face and how soft it feels, so compare very carefully. Look for soft and comfortable, unless you especially like having pressure headaches and don't mind looking like a very large octopus glommed on to your face.

Lack of 20-20 vision needn't cut into your viewing pleasure, but it does require a little more effort during equipment selection. Those who wear contact lenses can use them within their masks, taking on the risk that they'll swish out and float softly and invisibly down to the sea bed, perhaps to be found by a fossil hunter in the distant future, but certainly not by you. Use the disposable kind. Unless you use contacts, search for a correctable mask. Vision-correcting lens are available for many masks in 1/2 diopter increments.

parrotfish

If the mask you prefer doesn't offer standard correcting lenses, custom prescription lenses can be fitted to almost any mask. This costs more and takes longer. Even bifocals are available. We happen to prefer the comfortable prescription masks made by SeaVision which can be ordered with any custom correction. The cost is much like normal prescription lenses.

Mustaches create a mask leakage problem. As I like the look of a mustache, I have coped with this my entire adult life. Some advise the use petroleum jelly to make a more effective seal. That doesn't appeal to me since I go in and out of the water several times a day. It does help to choose a mask that rests high over the mouth and perhaps trim the top 1/8 inch or so off the center mustache, if it sticks up. Hair breaks the seal and allows water to seep into the mask slowly, so you'll still have to clear the mask occasionally.

Someone who has struggled with a leaky mask may prefer having a purge valve. There are some clever higher-end purge valve masks. The challenge is how to fit in a purge valve without making it harder to pinch your nose to equalize your ears when surface or scuba diving.

The conventional wisdom in Scuba is that purge valves are an unnecessary weak point. Nevertheless, there are experienced divers who use them. This isn't an issue snorkelers need worry about. If you find a purge valve mask that fits well, use it.

Mask Strap

The strap that comes with the mask is generally fine, but if you have your own mask and want it to slide on more easily, there's a comfortable strap available with adjustment by velcro. The back is made of wetsuit material – stretchy and soft. Cost is about $12 in dive shops. Since we get in and out so often, we happen to prefer this one to the regular strap, but it's a convenience for the frequent snorkeler rather than a necessity.

convict tang

Low Volume Masks

When you begin looking at masks, the variety can be bewildering. How can you figure out which design is best for you?

Inexpensive masks tend to have one large flat front glass. They're OK if the skirt of the mask fits you, although they're often a bit stiff and uncomfortable. They also tend to be far out from your face with a big air space. As you go up in price, the lenses tend to get smaller and closer to your eyes, as preferred by divers. There is a good Scuba reason for this. These are called "low volume" masks. They contain less airspace and so require less effort to clear when water gets in. They also press less against your face when you go deeper and the pressure rises (if you forget to blow higher pressure air in through your nose) and hence are more comfortable when diving.

For a snorkeler this is of little importance, but it still should be considered as you select your mask. Many snorkelers go on to do some surface diving, as well as Snuba or Scuba diving. When you dive down even 10', the water pressure is considerable. At 32', the air in your lungs and mask is compressed to half its volume, and unless you remember to blow some air into your mask through your nose, the pressure on your face can be most uncomfortable!

If your mask is flooded, which does happen occasionally, it is easier to clear out the water from a low volume mask. So, while it's not the most important factor, if everything else is equal, low volume is better.

Fins

The simplest fins are basic (usually black) enclosed foot fins. These are one-piece molded rubber and slip right on to your bare feet. For warm water, basic snorkeling, these inexpensive fins are fine. We own several kinds of fins and still often choose the one-piece foot fins for lightness and compact packing. They seem to last forever and are inexpensive ($15 – $25).

Why should anyone look further? Because it is possible to get better comfort and more thrust. Specialized fins are now made for higher performance. We tested three sets of fins, doing timed swims over a measured course. The basic fins discussed above went first. A set of fairly expensive, but rather soft, flexible strap-on fins cut the swim time by 20%, while ultra long, stiff-bladed foot-mount Cressi fins cut it by 40%! These long surface diving fins are, however, a little long and awkward to use for most surface snorkeling.

Opinions vary about the merits of flexible fin blades versus stiff blades. We've tested both for snorkeling, and we prefer light, thin, stiff blades, hands down. We also prefer fins that don't float, which isn't an issue with Scuba divers, but can reduce a snorkeler's efficiency if it holds the fins too high in the water.

You're better off with a medium blade foot fin for most snorkeling. Large diving fins are awkward for snorkeling, and require more leg strength than most non-athletes possess. The big diving fins do come in numerous shapes and colors, which some people are convinced will make them faster or perhaps more attractive. Speed is not the main aim of snorkeling, but has its uses. Faster fins do enable you to cover more territory and they also serve as excellent insurance in case you wander into a strong current. Unless it's absolutely certain that no current can carry you away, ALWAYS WEAR FINS!

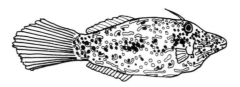

scrawled filefish

As you look at more advanced fins, they split into two attachment methods with pros and cons to each type. We own both and pick the best for a particular situation.

ENCLOSED FOOT — Your bare foot slides into a stretchy, integral molded rubber shoe.

Advantages — The lightest, most streamlined and fish-like fit. It probably is the most efficient at transmitting your muscle power to the blade. We prefer this type when booties are not required for warmth or safety.

Disadvantages — The fins must be closely fitted to your particular foot size. Some models may cause blisters. If you have to hike in to the entry site, you need separate shoes. This may preclude entering at one spot, and exiting elsewhere. If you hike over rough ground (a'a lava, for example) to get to your entry point, or the entry is over sharp coral or other hazards, these may not be the best choice.

STRAP-ON — Made for use with booties.

Advantages — Makes rough surface entry easy. Just hike to the entry point, head on into the water holding your fins in hand, lay back and pull on your fins. Exiting is just as easy. The bootie cushions your foot, making blisters unlikely. Widely used for Scuba.

Disadvantages — Less streamlined. The bootie makes your feet float up, so you may have trouble keeping your fins from breaking the surface.

No matter how good the fins, snorkeling for long hours may cause blisters – especially on the heel. No need to worry if you carry 3M Nexcare waterproof bandages. These little essentials will do the job and stay in place well when wet. Buy them at a major pharmacy before your trip – they can be hard to find in the islands.

Reef Shoes or Booties

Walking with bare feet on a'a (sharp lava) or coral can shred your feet in a quick minute. There are fine reef shoes available that are happy in or out of the water. These are primarily for getting there, or wading around, as they don't really work that well with strap-on fins. For the sake of the reef, don't actually walk on a reef with reef shoes, since each step kills hundreds of the little animals that make up the living reef.

Zip-on booties are widely used by divers and allow use of strap-on fins. They do float your feet – a disadvantage for snorkelers.

Keeping Time

One easy-to-forget item: a water-resistant watch. This needn't be expensive and is very useful for pacing yourself and keeping track of your sun exposure time.

"Water resistant" alone usually means that a little rain won't wreck the watch, but immersion in water may. When a designation like "to 10 meters" is added, it denotes added water-resistance; but the dynamic pressures from swimming increase the pressure, so choose 50 meters or greater rating to be safe even when snorkeling. Don't take a 50 meter watch Scuba diving, though – that requires 100-200 meter models.

Hawai'ian time is two hours earlier than Pacific Standard Time or three hours earlier than Pacific Daylight Time. Hawai'i doesn't observe Daylight Savings Time.

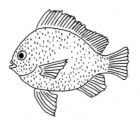

Hawai'ian damselfish

Body Suit

There are a variety of all-body suits that protect you from sun exposure and light abrasion, but provide no warmth. They are made from various synthetic fabrics – lycra and nylon being common. They cost much less than wetsuits and are light and easy to pack. We usually bring ours along as a sun protection alternative in warmer conditions. If you don't want to look like a F.O.B. (Fresh Off the Boat) tourist, with a shocking pink outline of your swimsuit, plan ahead about sun protection. You'll sleep better if you do too. And the fish will not miss all that sunscreen fouling their water.

Wetsuit

In Kaua'i average water temperature on the surface varies from a low of about 72° F in March to a high of about 80° F in September. If you happen to be slender, no longer young or from a moderate climate, this can seem cold. Sheltered bays and tidepools can be a bit warmer while deeper water can be surprisingly cold. Fresh water runoff can also make water cooler than you might expect. We've snorkeled in March when we swore it was not above 65° F off Kaua'i.

Regardless of the exact temperature, the water is cooler than your body. With normal exertion, your body still cools bit by bit. After awhile, perhaps 30-45 minutes, you start feeling a little chilly. Later you begin shivering and eventually hypothermia begins.

We like to snorkel for two or more hours sometimes. A thin wetsuit protects us from the sun while keeping us warm and comfortable. Off the rack suits are a bargain and fit most folks. Look for a snug fit at neck, wrists and ankles – if your suit is loose there, water will flow in and out, making you cold. If you have big feet and small ankles, get zippers on the legs if possible or you'll really have to struggle to remove the suit when it's wet.

Wetsuit wearers get added range and buoyancy. Wetsuit wearers hardly need a life jacket! Wearing a wetsuit, you can stay in the water without hypothermia for many hours – even in the winter. This could be comforting in the unlikely event that some strong current sweeps you off towards Fiji. There are few situations from which you can't rescue yourself if you're wearing a wetsuit and fins.

We recently discovered a new technology we like a lot: Henderson Gold Core wetsuits, made in Millville, New Jersey. The inside of this suit is coated with a gold-colored nylon that slides on like a breeze wet or dry, and the inner surface dries very quickly. The three millimeter-thick version is light, warm enough for Hawai'i snorkeling and has extra stretch so it's comfortable and easy to get on and off.

Even Gold Core slides poorly on skin with dried on sticky saltwater (as when you're getting in and out frequently on a multi-stop boat trip), though better than regular wetsuits. We found, however, that if you get wet first (in a beach shower, boat shower, or jumping in), Gold Core slides on like teflon.

Dave Barry once described putting on a wetsuit as like wrestling with an octopus. Not this one! No more hanging onto the shower while your buddy tries to pull the wetsuit off your ankles with a winch. If you can afford the extra cost, the suit is superb. We had ours custom-made with longer arms and legs, and no rubberized kneepads. We like our wetsuits sleek and flexible.

Swim Cap

If you have trouble with long hair tangling in your mask straps while snorkeling, get a lycra Speedo swim cap. It may look silly, but it works, and also protects your scalp from too many rays.

Snorkeling Vest

It is possible to buy inflatable vests made for snorkeling. Some guidebooks and stores promote them as virtually essential. We've taken excursions that require all snorkelers to wear one. Other excursions encourage the use of floatation "noodles" or kick boards – whatever it takes to make you comfortable.

Vests are hardly necessary in salt water for most people, but can be useful if you can't swim a lick or won't be willing to try this sport without it. There is a possible safety edge for kids or older folks. If you do get a vest, you can give it to another beginner after you get used to snorkeling. You will discover that it takes little effort to float flat in the water while breathing through a snorkel.

If you want extra flotation, consider using a light wetsuit instead. It simultaneously gives you buoyancy, sun and critter protection, and warmth.

Using the Hawai'ian Libraries

There is a great resource available on all the islands – one of the best bargains in Hawai'i.

For just $25, any Hawai'ian library will issue you a library card good for three years. This gives you full access to the rich and varied collections in the many local libraries. Believe us, if you take advantage of this, you'll be glad you did.

We make a stop at our local library soon after we arrive, checking out books on natural history, fish identification, Hawai'ian history and language, and much more. The "Hawai'iana" section in each library is a collection of books that include the above topics, and a good place to start.

You can check out a full range of videos for a week for just $1 each (one of the few things that cost extra). Don't forget to try some music CDs or tapes, too. If you're interested, you can look over USGS topographic maps. Copy machines are available at 10 cents per page.

All the libraries have internet terminals, and you can reserve an hour's session for free. Pick up your email and browse the web. Or sit in comfortable chairs and read an assortment of local newspapers and magazines.

Surface Diving Gear

For surface diving, bigger fins help your range. Those surreal-looking Cressi fins that seem about three feet long will take you down so fast you'll be amazed. You'll also be amazed how few suitcases are wide enough to accommodate them.

A long-fin alternative is to use a soft weight belt with from 2 to 4 pounds (more if you wear a wetsuit) – just enough to help you get under the surface without using up all your energy. As you descend, you become neutrally buoyant at about 15-20 feet so you don't have to fight popping up. Of course, the sword cuts two ways, since you must swim up under your own power in time to breathe.

Into the Water

Getting Started

Now that you've assembled a nice collection of snorkel gear, you're ready to go! On a sunny tropical morning you're down at the water's edge. Little one-foot waves slap the sand lightly, while a soft warm breeze takes the edge off the intensity of the climbing sun. It's a great day to be alive and out in the water.

Going snorkeling, it's better to have no suntan lotion on your face or hands. You sure don't want it washing into your eyes to make them burn and water. Wear a nice big hat instead. You applied lotion to your back before you left, so it had time to become effective. Then you washed off your hands and rinsed them well so the lotion couldn't contaminate your mask later.

Or you could do like we do, and skip all the lotion. Being outside as much as we are, and in and out of the water, we prefer to carefully cover up instead – we find too much lotion hard on our skin. Big broad hats like your boat captain wears help. Comfortable cotton cover-ups look good and are cool. Lycra body suits or wetsuits in the water let you stay in for as long as you wish. Do watch out for reflected light on long boat trips, which can sneak in and sizzle your tender face.

Checking Conditions

Take it nice and slow. Sit down and watch the waves for awhile. Check the slope of the beach. Consider whether there might be currents. Look for wave patterns, how big the biggest waves are and how far they wash up on the beach. When you see the pattern, you're ready to go. Set your gear down back well beyond the furthest watermarks on the sand. You don't want that seventh wave to sweep your gear away! Watch as long as it takes to be sure conditions aren't changing for the worse.

Gearing Up

Now defog the mask so that water vapor from your nose, or water leakage, won't bead up on your mask lens and spoil your view. There are two ways to defog.

The classic solution is: SPIT. Spit on the inside of your dry mask lens, and rub it all around with your sunscreen-free finger. Step into the water, just out beyond the stirred up sand, and dip up a mask full of clear saltwater. Thoroughly rub and rinse off that spit, and dump the mask. Now you have prepared a mask that should be fog-resistant for an average snorkel.

If you spit and polish, and still have fogging problems, there are several possible causes. Your mask may be gooped up with cosmetics, dried on saltwater residue or whatever other goo may be out there. A good cleaning with toothpaste may be in order (see Caring for Your Gear, page 192).

It's possible that you didn't actually wet all the surface with spit; perhaps because there were drops of water left on the lens. In that case, or if you just feel funny about spitting in your mask, you can use no-fog solution. No-fog solution for masks actually does work even better than spit. It comes in small, handy, inexpensive bottles that seem to last forever because you use only a few drops at a time. If you prefer to make your own, half baby shampoo and half water works fine.

Our favorite trick is to pre-apply no-fog solution to the dry masks an hour or more ahead and let it dry. When you get to the water, just rinse out the mask thoroughly. This seems to last a long time.

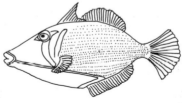

lei triggerfish

Getting Comfortable

After you rinse your mask, try its fit. Adjust the mask strap and snorkel until they're comfortable. Hold the snorkel in your mouth without tightening your jaws. It can be quite loose without falling out. Putting your mask on long before you enter the water can cause it to fog from your exertions

Getting Wet

Now retrieve your fins and walk back in the water, watching the waves carefully. NEVER turn your back on the ocean for long, lest a rogue wave sneak up on you and whack you good. The key is to stay alert and awake – especially on entry and exit.

Snorkeling is Easier than Swimming

Some folks never learn to snorkel because they're not confident as swimmers. This is an unnecessary loss because snorkeling is actually easier than swimming. We have maintained this to friends for years, and noted their doubtful looks. Recently, we came across a program in California that actually uses snorkeling as a tool to help teach swimming!

The Transpersonal Swimming Institute in California specializes in the teaching of adults who are afraid of the water. Local heated pools are used all year. But the warm, salty and buoyant ocean is the best pool of all.

Melon Dash, Director of TSI, takes groups of her students to Hawai'i where they begin by floating comfortably in the warm, salty water. At their own pace, they gradually learn to snorkel and feel comfortable in the water. For people further from California, a video called The Miracle Swimmer is available by mail.

"We have found that people cannot learn what to do with their arms and legs while they are afraid that they might not live."

With a steady air supply and not having to worry about breathing in water accidentally, they can relax and learn the arm and leg movements at ease. Happily, they soon discover there's nothing complicated about it!

In calm conditions and warm water, there need be no age limits and few physical limits for snorkeling.

Transpersonal Swimming Institute	(800) 723-7946
P.O. Box 6543	(510) 526-6000
Albany, CA 94706-0543	fax (510) 526-6091
Transwim@aol.com	www.conquerfear.com

If the bottom is sandy smooth, wade on out until you're about waist deep. Pull your mask on, making sure you remove any stray hair from under the skirt. Position the snorkel in your mouth and start breathing. You can practice this in a pool or hot tub.

Duck down in the water so you're floating and pull on your fins just like sneakers. Be sure no sand is trapped in the fins. Make a smooth turn to your stomach, pause to float and relax until you're comfortable, and you're off! Flip those fins and you have begun your re-entry into the sea.

As you float, practice steady breathing through the snorkel. Breathe slowly and deeply. People sometimes tense up at first and take short breaths. When this happens, you're only getting stale air from the snorkel rather than lots of fresh air from outside. If you ever feel tired or out of breath, don't take off your mask. Just stop as long as necessary, float, breathe easy and relax.

After you've become quite comfortable breathing this way, check how your mask is doing. Make sure it isn't leaking. Adjust the strap if needed. And keep adjusting until it's just right. Slide your snorkel strap to a comfortable position, with the tube pointing about straight up as you float looking down at about a 30° angle.

Swimming while snorkeling is easy once you've relaxed. No arms are required. What works best is to hold your arms straight back along your sides, keep your legs fairly straight and kick those fins slowly without bending your knees much. Any swimming technique will work, of course, but some are more tiring. Practice using the least amount of energy. Once you learn how to snorkel the easy way, you can use all the power you like touring large areas as if you were a migrating whale. But if you're breaking the surface with your fins, going "splash, plunk, splash", you're wasting energy. Be cool and smooth and quiet like a fish.

Clearing Your Mask

Eventually you will need to practice clearing your mask. The Scuba method: take a deep breath, then tip your head up, but with the mask still under the surface. Press your palm to the top of the mask against your forehead, or hold your fingers on the top of the mask and exhale through your nose. This forces water out the bottom of the mask.

Taking it Easy

Relax and try not to push yourself too hard. Experienced snorkelers may urge you on faster than you're comfortable because they've forgotten how it feels to get started. As your experience builds, you'll find it easy too. It's like learning to drive a car. Remember how even a parking lot seemed like a challenge? It helps to practice your beginning snorkeling in a calm easy place – with a patient teacher. With a little persistence, you'll soon overcome your fears and be ready. Don't feel like you should rush. Play around and have fun!

Knowing Your Limits

Have you heard the old saloon saying: "Don't let your mouth write checks that your body can't cover"?

Let's paraphrase this as "Don't let your ego take you places your body can't get you back from." Consider carefully how well-conditioned your legs are, so you'll have enough reserve to be able to make it back home, and then some in case of an emergency.

Snorkeling Alone

In your enthusiasm for the reef, you may wind up in this situation: your significant other prefers watching sports on ESPN to snorkeling one afternoon, and you're sorely tempted to just head out there alone. Don't do it. Snorkeling, done in buddy teams, is a pretty safe recreation, especially if conditions are favorable. Just as in Scuba diving, having a buddy along reduces the risk of a small problem becoming a big problem or even a fatal problem. We won't spell out all the bad things that could happen; we trust your imagination.

Pacing

When you're having a good time, it's easy to forget and overextend yourself. That next rocky point beckons, and then a pretty spot beyond that. Pretty soon, you're many miles from home and getting tired. Getting cold and overly tired can contribute to poor judgement in critical situations, making you more vulnerable to injury. Why risk turning your great snorkeling experience into a disaster? Learn your limits, and how to pace yourself.

Our favorite technique: If we plan on a one-hour snorkel, we watch the time and start heading back when we've been in the water 30 minutes. If the currents could run against us on the way back, we allow extra time/energy. We like to start by swimming against the current, making the trip home easy and quick.

Caring for Your Gear

You just had a great snorkeling experience – now you can thank the gear that helped make it possible, by taking good care of it.

Rinse and Dry

If there are beach showers, head right up and rinse off. Salt residue is sticky and corrosive. Rinse salt and sand off your wetsuit, fins, mask and snorkel before the saltwater dries. If you can, dry your gear in the shade. It's amazing how much damage sun can do to the more delicate equipment – especially the mask. When the sun odometer hits 100,000 miles, you can kiss those silicon parts goodbye.

Safety Inspections

Keep an eye on vulnerable parts after a few years (strap, snorkel-holder, buckles). Parts are usually easy to find in Hawai'i, but not in the middle of a snorkeling trip unless you're on a well-equipped boat.

If you use any equipment with purge valves, keep an eye on the delicate little flap valves, and replace them when they deteriorate. Masks and snorkels are useless when the valves give way. Remember that many snorkels now have a purge valve at the bottom.

Clean Your Mask

A mask needs a thorough cleaning between trips as well. Unless your mask instructions advise otherwise, use a regular, non-gel toothpaste to clean the lens inside and out, polishing off accumulated goo. Wash the toothpaste off with warm water, using your finger to clean it well.

Potter's angelfish

Hazards

Life just isn't safe. Snorkeling has a few hazards that you should know and avoid if possible. You already know the dangers of car and air travel, yet you mustered your courage and decided that a trip to Hawai'i was worth the risks. And you took reasonable precautions like buckling your seat belt. Well, if you use your noggin, you're probably safer in the water than while driving to get to the water.

Some people are hesitant to snorkel because they imagine meeting a scary creature in the water. But wouldn't you rather be able to see what's down there when you're swimming? We much prefer to see whatever you might step on, run into or encounter. The realities are seldom scary.

We don't think it makes sense to overemphasize certain lurid dangers (sharks!) and pay no attention to the more likely hazard of sunburn which causes more aggravation to tourists.

Sunburn

This is the worst medical problem you're likely to face – especially if you have the wrong ancestors. Use extra water-resistant sunblock in the water and always wear some kind of cover-up during the day. Some people need to avoid the sun entirely from 10 a.m. to 3 p.m., so that's a good excuse to go early and avoid the crowds. The top (or open) deck of a boat is a serious hazard to the easily-burned because bounced rays from the water will double your exposure. The best protection is covering up. Evidence mounts that sunscreen still allows skin damage even though it stops burning. Thanks to global warming, we all get more sun in a given hour than we did ten years ago.

When snorkeling, omit sunscreen on your face or hands, because you'll be sorry later if you get the stuff in your eyes. It can really sting and make it difficult to see well enough to navigate back to shore. To avoid using gallons of sunblock, some snorkelers wear lycra body suits. Others simply wear some old clothing.

Take an old sun hat to leave on the beach with your gear bag, especially if you have to hike midday across a reflective white beach. Take old sunglasses that are not theft-worthy. If you must leave prescription glasses on the beach, use your old ones. Kaua'i is a great place to find amazingly cheap sunglasses and flip-flops. For long hours in the sun, look into the better sunglasses that carefully filter all the most damaging rays.

Understanding Waves

Waves are travelling ripples in the water, mostly generated by wind blowing over large expanses of water. Having considerable energy, the waves keep going until something stops them. They may travel many thousands of miles before dissipating that energy. Here is the wellspring of the breaking surf. That beautiful surf can also be the biggest danger facing snorkelers.

Take time to sit on a high point and watch the waves approaching the coast, and you will see patterns emerge. Usually there is an underlying groundswell from one direction, waves that may have originated in distant storms. This is the main source of the rhythmical breaking waves, rising and falling in size in noticeable patterns. Sometimes there will be a smaller secondary groundswell from another direction. Often, there will be a series of small waves, followed by one or more larger waves, and the cycle repeats. Pay attention to the patterns and it will be less likely that you'll get caught by surprise.

Local winds add extra energy in their own directions. In Hawai'i, snorkeling is usually easiest in the mornings, before the daily winds create chop and larger waves.. Most excursions head out early to make sure they have smooth sailing and calm snorkeling. Sometimes afternoon excursions are offered at reduced prices to compensate for expected rougher conditions.

Occasionally a set of larger waves or a single large rogue wave comes in with little or no warning. A spot that was protected by an offshore reef suddenly has breaking waves. This change can happen while you're out, and make coming back difficult.

Our single worst moment in many years of snorkeling and diving was at Po'ipu Beach Park in Kaua'i after Hurricane Iniki had scattered boulders throughout the beach. We had no problem snorkeling around the boulders in a light swell, protected by reef further out. Suddenly much larger waves crossed the reef and began breaking over us, sweeping everyone back and forth against the boulders.

Since then we have been extra careful to avoid potentially hazardous situations. We always take time to study the waves before entering and ponder what would happen if they suddenly grew much larger, and what our strategy would be. Sometimes we just head for a calmer beach.

Rip Currents

Hawai'i does not have large barrier reefs to intercept incoming waves. Few of Kaua'i's beaches are well-protected from powerful ocean currents – especially in the winter or during storms.

Waves breaking against a shore push volumes of water up close to the shore. As this piles up, it has to flow back to the ocean, and often flows sideways along the shore until it reaches a convenient, often deeper-bottomed, exit point. There, a fast, narrow river of water flows out at high speed. Rip currents, which can carry swimmers out quickly, are of limited duration by their very nature and usually stop no more than 100 yards out.

Sometimes it's possible to swim sideways, but often it's better to simply ride it out. Don't panic. Although the current might be very strong, it won't take you far or drown you, unless you exhaust yourself by swimming against it. It's very easy to float in salt water until help arrives – assuming you're at a beach where someone can see you. Don't try to swim in through waves where there's any chance of being mashed on lava rocks or coral. Don't swim against the current to the point of exhaustion. When in doubt, float and conserve energy.

Even at the most protected beaches all the water coming in must get out, so when swells are up, there's a current somewhere. Big waves beyond the breakwater may seem harmless, but the more water comes in, the more must get out. This is a good reason to ALWAYS wear fins.

Rip currents should not be confused with offshore currents, such as the infamous "Tahiti Express". There are some major flows of water offshore that can be faster than you can swim, even with fins. Do be alert and careful if you swim out beyond rocky points. Or send us a postcard from Tahiti.

Hypothermia

Open ocean water is always cooler than your body, and it cools you off more rapidly than the air. With normal exertion, your body still cools bit by bit. After awhile (perhaps 30-45 minutes) most of us start feeling chilly. Later, shivering begins. When your temperature drops even further, hypothermia sets in. When your body temperature has dropped enough, your abilities to move and even think become impaired.

We used to think hypothermia was just an interesting concept, until it happened to us after a long snorkel in some unusually cold water. We were shivering, but having a great time, and snorkeled on and on. Fortunately, we noticed the decrease in our co-ordination and headed in while we still could. You'd have laughed to see us stumbling clumsily out of the waves. We headed straight for the nearest jacuzzi. As we warmed up, our limbs tingled like fizzy water was going through our veins.

One of the first symptoms of hypothermia is poor judgement. Buddies can watch out for each other better than you can watch out for yourself alone – one example of the benefits of having a partner. Check up on each other often in cold conditions.

As soon as you are aware that you're cold, it's time to plan your way back. When shivering starts, you should get out of the water. Be particularly careful in situations requiring all your judgement and skill to be safe, especially when diving, night snorkeling, dealing with waves, or when anticipating a difficult exit from the water.

In Kaua'i, it's usually easy to warm up rapidly since the air temperature is fairly warm at sea level. Even without hypothermia, it's good to warm up between snorkels. If you came by car, it will probably be nicely solar-heated by the time you return.

Sea Urchins

Probably the most common critter injury is stepping on a spiny sea urchin and walking away with lots of spines under your skin. The purple-black spiny sea urchins with long spines tend to appear in groups and favor shallow water, so watch carefully if you see even one. Full-foot flippers or booties help a lot, but don't guarantee protection. Watch where you put your hands – especially in shallow water.

While many folks recommend seeing a doctor for urchin spine slivers, others prefer to just let the spines fester and pop out weeks later. Remove as much spine as you can. Vinegar (or other acidic liquid) will make it feel better. Soaking in Epsom salts helps and the small spines will dissolve in a few weeks, but see a doctor at any sign of infection.

Barracudas

The great barracuda can grow to two meters, has sharp teeth and strong jaws, and swims like a torpedo. For years Judy has removed earrings before swimming after hearing rumors that they attract barracuda, but we've uncovered absolutely no confirming reports of severed ear-ringed ears.

Barracudas are capable of seriously injuring a swimmer so should be taken seriously. Those teeth are just as sharp as they look. Barracudas appear to have attitude, and apparently sometimes do. Our own preference is to respect their territory and allow them some space. Other varieties of barracuda such as the Heller's appear more innocuous.

Once a five-foot great barracuda swam directly beneath us in the Caribbean and appeared annoyed that we were invading his home territory (or so we thought from the fierce look on his face). A calm and steady German surgeon headed up the nearest rocks as if she could fly. The rest of us snorkeled by him repeatedly with no problem, but didn't appreciate the look he gave us. We later came to realize that they always look grumpy, but seldom bite, like some folks you may know. Perhaps the bigger danger comes from eating the delicious barracuda meat, sometimes containing ciguatera, which is toxic to humans.

great barracuda

Portuguese Man-of-War

The Portuguese man-of-war floats on top, looking like a sailfin one to four inches in size, with long stinging filaments that are quite painful. Stay out of the water if you see one. Even avoid dead ones on the sand! They're very pretty in lovely shades of purple, but can cause severe pain.

Vinegar or unseasoned meat tenderizer helps ease the sting and helps stop the release of venom from the stinging cells if tentacles are clinging to you. Use wet sand as a last resort. If you feel ill, see a doctor right away. If jellyfish are present, locals will know which ones are harmful. Jellyfish have seldom been a problem for us in Hawai'i. In all our years in the water in Hawai'i, we've only been stung by a Portuguese man-of-war once.

Rays

Sting rays prefer to avoid you, but hang out on the bottom where they're easy to step on. They prefer resting in calm water that is slightly warmer than the surrounding area – just the areas favored by people for swimming. Step on them and they may sting you, so the injury is usually to the foot or ankle. They can inflict a serious or painful sting to people – especially children. It's best to get immediate first aid and follow up with medical assistance.

In this case snorkelers have an advantage over swimmers because snorkelers can see sting rays and easily avoid them. In Maui we've seen them swim between children's legs in shallow water at Kapalua Bay and were amazed to see how adept the rays were at avoiding people.

Manta rays don't sting, but they're much larger. They are often six to eight feet across weighing several hundred pounds. They maneuver beautifully, so don't pose any danger. With a little luck, you'll be able to see one of these beautiful creatures.

manta ray

31

Poisonous Fish

Lionfish (also called turkeyfish) and scorpionfish have spines which are very poisonous. Don't step on or touch them! Their poison can cause serious pain and infection or allergic reaction, so definitely see a doctor if you have a close, personal encounter with one. Fins or booties can help protect your tender feet.

Scorpionfish can blend in so well along the bottom in shallow water that they're easy to miss. Turkeyfish, though, are colorful and easy to spot. Since these fish are not abundant in Hawai'i, they are treasured sightings. You are not likely to encounter one in casual snorkeling.

Hawai'ian turkeyfish

Eels

Eels are rarely aggressive and often tamed by divers. Most do possess a formidable array of teeth, which should be avoided. An eel bite can definitely cause serious bleeding requiring prompt medical attention. Another good reason not to snorkel alone!

Eels are fascinating and easy to find in Hawai'i. Count on eels to make every effort to avoid you, so there's no need to panic at the sight of one – even if it's swimming freely. Eels aren't interested in humans as food, but they do want to protect themselves and can usually do so with ease by slipping away into the nearest hole. Do we need to tell you to keep your hands out of crevices in the coral?

leopard moray eel

Cone Shells

The snails inside these pretty black and brown-decorated shells can fire a poisonous dart. The venom can cause a serious reaction or even death – especially to allergic persons. If in doubt, head for a doctor. If you never pick up underwater shells, you won't have any problem.

cone shell

Drowning

Not likely to happen to you, but we want to help you become so alert and prepared that you have a safe vacation.

We looked up the statistics for the past 30 years, and they are both comforting and cautionary. Only 6-7 folks drown each year in Kaua'i. A much lower number than fatalities from auto wrecks, industrial accidents, or probably even accidents around the home.

A couple things stand out about who are the victims. Three out of four victims are visitors. Not too surprising, since you assume locals are more aware of the hazards. But nine out of ten are males, mostly 20 to 50 years old! You'd think this would be a low-risk group.

What leads these guys to get into a dangerous situation? Well, some guys just can't help overrating their athletic prowess, and perhaps underestimate the power of the ocean.

Some locations seem distinctly more hazardous. Hanakapi'ai Beach, first stop in on the Kalalau trail, is the leader. Make that tiring, hot hike, and then that water looks so refreshing! Then the riptide sweeps you out, and the rest is history.

Wailua/Lydgate is second. It's very unlikely the victims were swimming in the protected pond in Lydgate Park that we recommend. It's the surf-pounded beach areas that are the real hazard here. Lumahai is third, with Polihale, Po'ipu, and Kapa'a trailing.

It's easy to swim and snorkel in Kaua'i safely. Improve your odds by picking protected beaches when the surf is pounding. Don't overestimate your stamina. Perhaps you might follow our personal rule: always wear fins when swimming in the open ocean in Hawai'i!

Sharks

Sharks are seldom a problem for snorkelers. In Hawai'i the modest number of verified shark attacks have mostly occurred off O'ahu with tiger sharks the major perpetrator, and surfers the major targets. Sharks often hunt in very murky river runoff, but most snorkelers avoid these conditions anyway.

We have read that you're more likely to be killed by a pig than a shark. We take great comfort in that, as I'm sure you do, too; though we've quit eating bacon just in case.

Some people will suggest you can pet, feed or even tease certain types of shark. We personally would give sharks a bit of respect and leave them entirely in peace. Most sharks are well-fed on fish and not all that interested in well-oiled tourists, but it's hard to tell by looking at a shark whether it has had a bad day.

Sharks usually feed late in the day or at night, causing some people to prefer to enjoy the water more in the morning or midday. If you're in an area frequented by sharks, this might be good to keep in mind. We must admit that we snorkel at any hour, and occasionally night snorkel. The few sharks we have seen have all been midday.

In Kaua'i, with luck, you might possibly see sandbar, black-tip, white-tip or even hammerhead sharks – more often in deep water sites like 'Ahukini Landing or Hanalei Bay.

reef shark

I Like to Watch

"For some reason, the barracuda don't seem scary, any more than the ray does. For some reason, none of this seems scary. Even the idea of maybe encountering a smallish s___k doesn't seem altogether bad.

It's beginning to dawn on me that all the fish and eels and crabs and shrimps and plankton who live and work down here are just too busy to be thinking about mc.

I'm a traveller from another dimension, not really a part of their already event-filled world, not programmed one way or another – food or yikes – into their instinct circuits. They have important matters to attend to, and they don't care whether I watch or not. And so I watch."

– Dave Barry

Snorkeling Sites

Where are those big beautiful fish?

Kaua'i, with an abundance of sandy beaches, has many long stretches of fringing reef which provide snorkeling on all sides of the island. With this much reef, the snorkeling is often better than the swimming. The reef here is more developed than at any of the other main Hawai'ian islands because Kaua'i has been around the longest.

The Garden Isle is considerable less developed than the other islands, and has a smaller population. No other island has quite the lush tropical beauty of Kaua'i. It's lush for a reason – ample rainfall! Come prepared for the weather to be unpredictable with chances of very heavy rain and wind. Often you can snorkel with no problem in spite of the weather by driving to another beach that is drier or less choppy. Most of the coast is within easy driving distance, except for the Na Pali Coast, where you won't find any roads at all.

The site section begins at the end of the highway in the far northwest, where the Na Pali coast begins. Ke'e Beach and Tunnels are two excellent and scenic spots along this green and lush far corner of Kaua'i. Here, rivers from the nearly high mountains emerge at sandy beaches with broad reefs offshore. Winter brings huge waves from the north to this part of the island, making the beaches off-limits for nearly any sport except surfing. Rain showers are intense, but may last only a short time. Longer storms bring murky run-off to the bays. But the sun always comes back, and when conditions are favorable, these gorgeous northwest beaches are glorious.

Princeville offers small secluded beaches (usually about 200 feet below the bluff) and plenty of luxurious condominium accommodations nearby. The hikes to get to them are pretty and pleasant, and well worth the effort.

Northern Kaua'i has many long sandy beaches. A few, such as two-mile long 'Anini and the Tunnels area are well-protected by a large fringing reef. Others, like Kauapea, offer no protection from swells and surf. Still, when surf is low, the snorkeling is worthwhile at these beaches.

The eastern side of Kaua'i is exposed to the heavy east swell nearly all year. While these beaches often have broad, low reefs, the relentless swells from the east make them difficult and dangerous during much of the year. Two or three weeks a year, they flatten, and are calm and easy to snorkel. If you are lucky enough to be there when that happens, jump in! At all other times, be cautious.

There are some exceptions. Lydgate Park (completely protected by a man-made breakwater) and Kalapaki (inside of Nawiliwili Bay) are almost always safe. Anahola Beach Park offers some protection from swells at Anahola Bay's south end.

The southeast contains some of Kaua'i's least developed spots (at least for the time being) in the Maha'ulepo area near Poipu, where sand dunes and isolation are both appealing and easy to reach. This area is quite windswept, and some days may be better-suited for flying kites than picnicking.

The popular Po'ipu area in the south provides plenty of snorkeling beaches, the widest assortment of accommodations, more hours of sun and less rainfall. Po'ipu has quite a variety of snorkeling sites within easy driving distance, from small to large, calm to challenging. Choose the broad sandy beach shared by the Sheraton Hotel and the Kiahuna Plantation, or try slightly less scenic Koloa Landing or Ho'ai Bay. The south is a good bet in winter, when the north is likely to be much rougher and wetter.

As the highway continues counterclockwise, it reaches the big western beaches. Barking Sands beaches stretch for miles. Most of the Hawai'ian islands have the best snorkeling on the protected leeward southwest and west sides.. Kaua'i's western beaches, however, tend to be very rough, due to their exposure to the vast Pacific Ocean. When swells roll in from the northeast, they wrap around and affect western Kaua'i.. Prevailing swell and currents travel around Kaua'i and converge off Barking Sands, making some impressive large roller coaster swells. Snorkeling and swimming is usually dangerous along this coast. Salt Pond Beach Park is an exception due to its natural breakwater.

Five miles past the far western end of the paved highway lies secluded Polihale Beach, on the southern flank of the rugged Na Pali coast. Several small reef-fringed beaches can provide good snorkeling off this dramatic coast, when the weather cooperates. All must be accessed by excursion or kayak, unless you plan a year or more ahead and secure a hiking permit, and then make the long, strenuous hike from the northern trailhead.

Excursions from Hanalei and Port Allen both offer trips to the Na Pali coast as well as Ni'ihau Island and Lehua Island, a pristine volcanic crater about a mile north of Ni'ihau.

Because swell direction and exact angle of each beach is so important in Kaua'i, we've made sure to draw each map with north at the top. We've also listed them in clockwise direction.

Snorkel Site Index Map

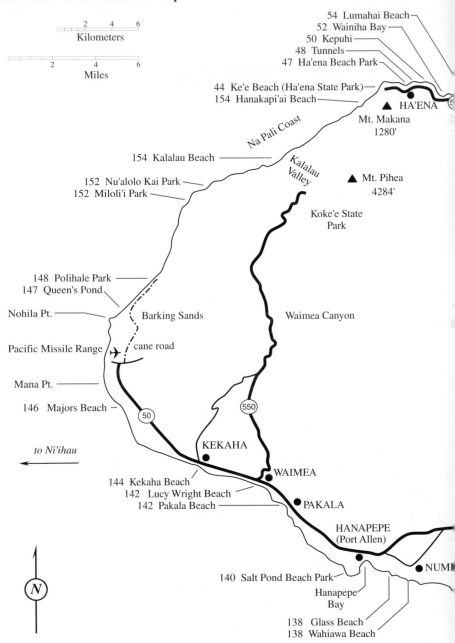

Kilometers
2   4   6

Miles
2   4   6

54 Lumahai Beach
52 Wainiha Bay
50 Kepuhi
48 Tunnels
47 Ha'ena Beach Park
44 Ke'e Beach (Ha'ena State Park)
154 Hanakapi'ai Beach

HA'ENA

Mt. Makana
1280'

Na Pali Coast

154 Kalalau Beach

Kalalau Valley

152 Nu'alolo Kai Park
152 Miloli'i Park

Mt. Pihea
4284'

Koke'e State Park

148 Polihale Park
147 Queen's Pond

Nohila Pt.

Barking Sands

Waimea Canyon

Pacific Missile Range

cane road

Mana Pt.

146 Majors Beach

50

550

to Ni'ihau

KEKAHA

144 Kekaha Beach
142 Lucy Wright Beach
142 Pakala Beach

WAIMEA

PAKALA

HANAPEPE
(Port Allen)

NUM

140 Salt Pond Beach Park

Hanapepe
Bay

138 Glass Beach
138 Wahiawa Beach

N

38

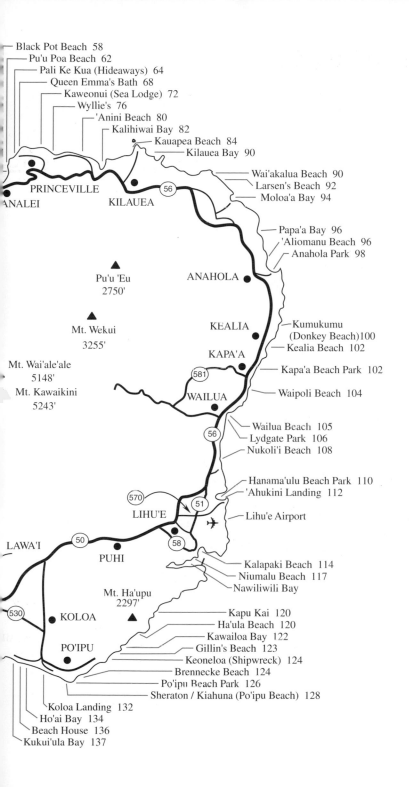

Sites at a Glance

	SNORKELING	ENTRY	SANDY BEACH	RESTROOM	SHOWERS	PICNIC AREA	SCENIC	SHADE
Ke'e Beach	A	1	•	•	•	•	•	•
Tunnels	A	1	•	•	•	•	•	•
Kepuhi Beach	B	1-3	•				•	•
Lumahai Beach	C	1-2	•				•	•
Hanalei beaches	B	1	•	•	•	•	•	•
Pu'u Poa (Princeville)	B	1	•	•	•	•	•	•
Pali Ke Kua (Hideaways)	B	2	•				•	•
Queen Emma's Bath	A	1					•	
Kaweonui (Sea Lodge)	A	1-2	•				•	•
'Anini Beach	C	1	•	•	•	•	•	•
Kalihiwai Bay	C	1-2	•		•		•	•
Kauapea (Secret Beach)	C	1-3	•				•	•
Larsen's Beach	C	3	•				•	•
Moloa'a Bay	B	1-2	•				•	•
Anahola Bay	B	1-2	•	•	•	•	•	•
Kapa'a Beach Park	C	1-2	•	•	•	•	•	•
Lydgate Beach Park	A	1	•	•	•	•	•	•
'Ahukini Landing	B	1						
Kalapaki Beach	B	1-2	•	•	•	•	•	•
Maha'ulepu beaches	B	1-2	•					•
Po'ipu State Park	B	1-2	•	•	•	•	•	•
Sheraton/Kiahuna	B	1-2	•	•	•	•	•	•
Koloa Landing	A	1						
Ho'ai Bay	A	1-2	•					•
Beach House	A	1-2	•	•	•			•
Salt Pond Beach	B	1	•	•	•	•	•	•
Polihale Beach Park	C	1-3	•	•	•	•	•	•
Lehua Island	A+	1					•	

A	Excellent	1	Easy
B	Good	2	Moderate
C	Fair	3	Difficult

PAGE	MAP PAGE	NOTES
44	45	tiny cove, spectacular location, popular, don't miss
48	49	snorkel at Tunnels, facilities at Ha'ena, tops when calm
50	53	good in summer, large reef, access around private homes
54	55	no coral, but some fish, dangerous when north swell, lovely
51	50	better for swimming, winter can bring huge waves
56	57	room to explore if calm, turtles, 171 steps down
64	65	very steep hike down cliff, shallow inner reef
68	69	enchanting small natural pool at base of cliffs
72	73	high tide necessary, worth hike down cliffs, secluded
80	81	high tide necessary, vast shallow inner reef to explore
82	83	pretty, somewhat protected bay, with swimming & kayaking
84	85	beautiful, long beach, variable conditions, pleasant hike in
92	93	rarely calm enough, long fringing reef, too shallow inside
94	95	pretty & lush valley, walk to ends of beach to snorkel
98	99	high tide best, lovely spot, room to explore when calm
102	103	often too rough, long beach with several possible sites
106	107	easiest snorkel in all Hawai'i, tops for beginners, big fish
112	113	deep water, experts only, big fish & sharks
114	115	big sheltered beach, calmer than most of the east
120	121	snorkeling safest between Kawailoa & Gillin's, secluded
126	127	popular, small, boulder habitat, avoid if heavy south swell
128	129	well-protected area, room to explore, long beach
132	133	excellent & calm, no beach, facilities or crowds
134	135	shallow entry, but good snorkeling & turtle hang-out
136	135	excellent variety, usually calm, uncrowded
140	141	usually very calm within protective breakwater, large fish
148	145	remote, uncrowded, often much too dangerous
156	157	back of volcanic crater, clear, steep drop-off, excursion only

Northwest Area

Picturesque beaches with a backdrop of towering mountains have made this lush, green corner of Kaua'i the location of choice as a backdrop for many movies. From Ke'e Beach, at the far end of the road, to Hanalei Bay, you'll find some of Kaua'i's most beautiful scenery. Highway 56 becomes a two-land road at Hanalei and proceeds west as Highway 560 over seven one-lane bridges as it winds through the northwest to the rugged and impassible Na Pali coast.

The Hanalei to Ha'ena area is the quietest and least developed corner of Kaua'i, where you'll find no big hotels, condos, golf courses or even supermarkets. The quiet little town of Hanalei has the only shopping in the area. You will find scattered homes near the narrow corridor of Highway 560 and plenty of sand beaches with several offshore reefs. Rains can be heavy here (to say the least) with over 500 inches falling up on top of Mount Wai'ale'ale, sending hundreds of narrow waterfalls cascading down the mountains and toward the sea. Winter storms from the North Pacific bring huge waves to this area, so snorkeling is usually better in the summer.

Conditions change often, though, so come prepared for any kind of seas. For a snorkeler, that means knowing which beaches are likely to be safe and enjoyable. It also means knowing that all water sports can be interrupted quite suddenly. Most of the heavy rains only last about ten minutes and are quite warm, so these you can wait out. While heavy rain itself needn't bother a snorkeler, the brown run-off from the rivers after major downpours will certainly do a job on the visibility of the water. When rains settle in, you'll probably need to snorkel elsewhere.

Kaua'i is a fairly small island, so this gorgeous area is easy to reach from the major tourist areas. The drive is green and relaxing: only ten miles from Princeville, half an hour from Kapa'a, and about an hour from Po'ipu (unless you hit rush hour traffic). Come when you have plenty of time to relax and enjoy the snorkeling as well as the many wonderful attractions, such as the Limahuli Botanical Gardens. No permit is required to hike the first stretch of the Kalalau Trail, and it makes a spectacular day hike.

Except for the Hanalei Colony Resort, the only accommodations available are in numerous private beach rental homes. Most of these are found on the ocean side (makai) of Highway 560. Renting one of these houses makes a great jungle vacation. Jungles have mosquitoes and ants, so bring repellent.

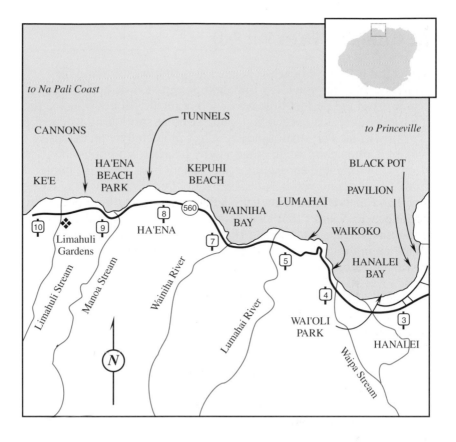

to Na Pali Coast

to Princeville

CANNONS

TUNNELS

KE'E

HA'ENA
BEACH
PARK

KEPUHI
BEACH

BLACK POT

PAVILION

10

9

Limahuli
Gardens

8

HA'ENA

560

WAINIHA
BAY

LUMAHAI

WAIKOKO

7

HANALEI
BAY

5

Limahuli Stream

Manoa Stream

Wainiha River

Lumahai River

4

WAI'OLI
PARK

3

HANALEI

Waipa Stream

N

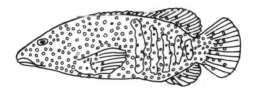

peacock grouper

43

Ke'e Beach (Ha'ena State Park)

Delightful little Ke'e beach is located at the far western end of Highway 560 after you cross Limahuli Stream. Come here for the scenic drive, the perfect little cove with dramatic Mount Makana in the background, lush vegetation, and excellent snorkeling when seas are fairly calm. The small sandy beach is protected by an extensive reef, so is often calm when other nearby beaches are impossible. Both swimming and snorkeling are excellent here, entry is simple from the sand, and you'll find such beauty that it's easy to stay all day. The Kalalau Trail along the Na Pali coast begins here at the left of the beach. A short trail also leads from the beach to a nearby house site, terraces, and an old Hawai'ian hula heiau, where the views are nothing short of spectacular. We highly recommend Ke'e Beach at any time of the year except after unusually heavy rains.

Novice snorkelers should stay within the small bay taking care to stay well away from the deep left channel, where currents can sweep you toward rugged Na Pali coast. Snorkeling is modest within the sandy bay, but the beautiful setting and some bright reef fish will please most beginners.

More experienced snorkelers will prefer to explore over the shallow reef on the right side. When conditions permit (especially in the summer), you can skim the reef along a shallow channel on the right to the outer edge where turtles abound (see map, page 45). High tide is the time to come if you want to snorkel over the reef. The tides in Kaua'i only swing about two feet, but it makes a big difference here. Low tide will give you only a claustrophobic one-foot clearance in spots, while high will provide about three feet. When big waves are crashing against the outer edge of the reef, all snorkelers should stay within the cove.

Ke'e Beach is located within 230-acre Ha'ena State Park, which is not to be confused with nearby Ha'ena Beach Park. You'll find a large parking lot, picnic areas, lifeguard, portapotties, and ever-present wild chickens. There's plenty of parking if you don't mind a short hike from the parking lot, but the park is getting very popular, so come early to be sure of getting a spot. Plan to stay awhile and thoroughly enjoy this incredible spot. For a pretty short hike, take the trail at the left side of the beach, past an old building site and wander up to the heiau reputed to be the birthplace of Hawai'ian hula. It's a rocky trail and a bit steep, but not far. From the terraces you can look out on the Na Pali coast and back to the reef at Ke'e Beach. An even steeper trail continues down to the next little beach west of Ke'e, where you'll probably find no crowds at all. Do not

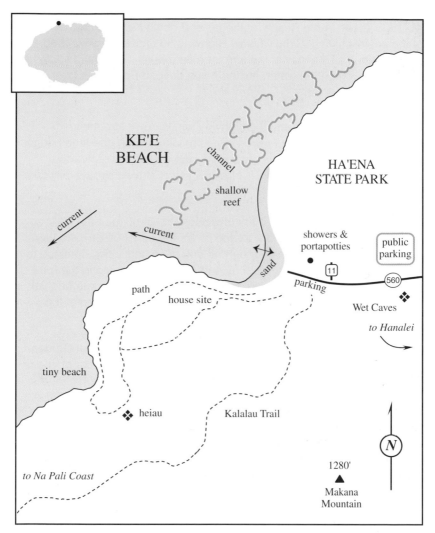

KE'E
BEACH

HA'ENA
STATE PARK

channel

shallow
reef

current

current

sand

showers &
portapotties

public
parking

11

560

path

house site

parking

Wet Caves

to Hanalei

tiny beach

heiau

Kalalau Trail

N

to Na Pali Coast

1280'

Makana
Mountain

swim or snorkel at this beach because a strong current sweeps to the
left all along the coast beyond Ke'e Beach.

The name Ha'ena means "red hot" and may have come from the
ancient Hawai'ian practice of throwing burning hollow sticks from
the top of Mount Makana. Look up and imagine what an enchanting
sight it must have been to see "fireworks" raining down from the top
of this steep mountain cloaked in greenery.

This rugged and out-of-the-way corner of Kaua'i was discovered by
the hippies in the '70s, who gathered together on land owned by a
brother of actress Liz Taylor. Strings of hippie-gathered puka shells
created quite a fashion craze. Hawai'ians of Ni'ihau have continued
this tradition, making some exquisite and expensive shell necklaces.

GETTING THERE Ke'e Beach, at the far end of the Kuhio Highway, is one of the easiest to find. Simply follow Highway 56 until it becomes 560, then continue all the way to the end (at mile marker 10), where you're a stone's throw from the water. It's ten miles beyond Princeville (see map, page 45).

As you pass Princeville and the highway winds down into the lush Hanalei Valley, it narrows to two lanes, crossing seven one-lane bridges where traffic must yield. Relax and enjoy the view if you're headed against the flow of traffic. This is Hawai'i, where drivers are usually courteous, so you'll get your turn.

You will pass Ha'ena Beach Park on your right. Continue until you see the sign for Ha'ena State Park as you cross the Limahuli Stream, then park in the large dirt lot on your right. If you're feeling lucky, continue to the end of the road, where you may find a parking spot along the road just steps from the beach. As Ke'e Beach becomes ever more popular, you'll probably prefer to avoid the congested traffic at the end of the road.

Just before entering the park, you will pass Limahuli Botanical Garden on your left. You might want to stop here for a self-guided tour of one of the most beautiful tropical gardens in the world.

Cannons (Ha'uwa)

This broad reef extends from Ke'e Beach in the west to Ha'ena Beach Park in the east and is called Cannons (and sometimes Ha'uwa). Most of the year this area is better for divers than snorkelers as the reef is shallow, the waves rough and the currents strong. It does provide arches and caves for the most experienced snorkeler on a calm day. Entrance is sometimes possible from Ke'e Beach to the west at high tide or from the sand at Ha'ena Beach Park to the east.

When surf is down and tide is up, the area nearest Ke'e offers relatively safe snorkeling. Avoid the far north of this reef at all times because the offshore current can easily sweep you toward the Na Pali coast.

Showers, restrooms, and picnic tables are all available at nearby Ha'ena Beach Park in the east and Ke'e Beach in the west.

GETTING THERE   Park in the Ha'ena Beach Park lot on the makai (towards the water) side of Highway 560 at mile marker 9 (see map, page 49). Then, cross the sand to the left to snorkel the Cannons reef extending out from the western end of the beach..

Alternatively, park at Ke'e Beach, then snorkel to the right across the reef. Continue toward Cannons only when conditions are favorable.

Ha'ena Beach Park   (Maniniholo)

Not to be confused with Ha'ena State Park. This park is located a short drive to the east on the makai (towards the water) side of Highway 560. The park offers camping, a broad sandy beach with a shallow stream near the center, showers, restrooms, and picnic tables, so it's a handy spot to stop after a day at Ke'e Beach. Parking is plentiful in the lot nearby.

You can also hike a quarter mile along the sand to your right (east) to get to Tunnels. There are closer entrances to Tunnels, but they sometimes fill in the middle of the day, so keep this parking area in mind. It's really not a long hike. Besides, at Ha'ena Beach Park you'll have a shower waiting when you return from snorkeling.

Swimming is good at the park and you can snorkel, but it's mostly sandy beach in the center, so you'll see much more at Tunnels to the right. In rough winter swells, the center can be particularly dangerous since it has no protecting reef directly in front.

Along the highway, you'll find Wai'akapala'e and Wai'akanaloa (Wet and Dry Caves). You might want to check them out while you're up in the area.

GETTING THERE   Ha'ena Beach Park is located on the makai (ocean) side of Highway 560 at mile marker 9 (see map, page 49). You will see a couple of dirt parking lots along the highway, with camping and picnicking nearby. Although the park is visible from the highway, it's easy to pass by.

This is a low-key beach with visitors spread over about a half mile of sand. While there is swimming in front, the better snorkeling entry is at Tunnels, which requires a quarter-mile hike across sand to the right. Snorkeling and swimming in front of Ha'ena Beach Park should be limited to very calm seas because a strong current here pulls to the left.

Tunnels (Makua Beach)

When surf is fairly low (especially likely during the summer), Tunnels is Kaua'i's premier snorkeling destination. The large horseshoe-shaped reef has an outer edge that catches the pounding waves. An inner reef is then available for easy snorkeling within the natural lagoon-like area – providing that storm waves aren't pounding all the way to shore.

No facilities are available at Tunnels, but nearby Ha'ena Beach Park offers showers, restrooms and picnic tables. There is plenty of space on the sand near the Tunnels reef with large shade trees along the edge of the beach.

The most convenient parking for Tunnels is either along the highway or along the little entrance road (see map, page 49), but both tend to fill early. If you arrive in the middle of day, you may need to park at Haena Beach Park and walk a quarter mile to your right (east) on sand to get to the Tunnels area. The river is usually only inches deep where it crosses the sand.

Snorkeling entry is easy from the wide sand beach, especially where we've marked on our map. Avoid the shallow areas with reef and rocks right up to the beach edge. Beginners should stay close to shore following the inner reef. Even in the best weather, there tends to be a slight current toward the left. Be careful not to drift too far. You can always enter further up the beach to the right and simply drift slowly along the reef and exit closer to the left edge of the reef. This inner area ranges from about three to thirty-feet deep with channels, caverns and, yes, tunnels.

More experienced snorkelers will want to explore closer to the outer reef (depending on currents and swell). When calm enough, this reef has plenty of room to explore. In places it drops off to about 50-70 feet. The outer reef is our favorite. We've seen turtles, huge cornetfish, parrotfish, banded filefish, Moorish idols, bird wrasses, rockmover wrasses, big chubs and jacks, many kinds of butterflyfish and much more.

Tunnels is a must-see when the weather co-operates. Stay out of water when huge waves kick in, which they often do in the winter.

GETTING THERE From Princeville, take Highway 560 (Kuhio Highway) through the town of Hanalei, past Hanalei Bay and past the Hanalei Colony Resort. Watch the mile markers carefully so you can park close to Tunnels.

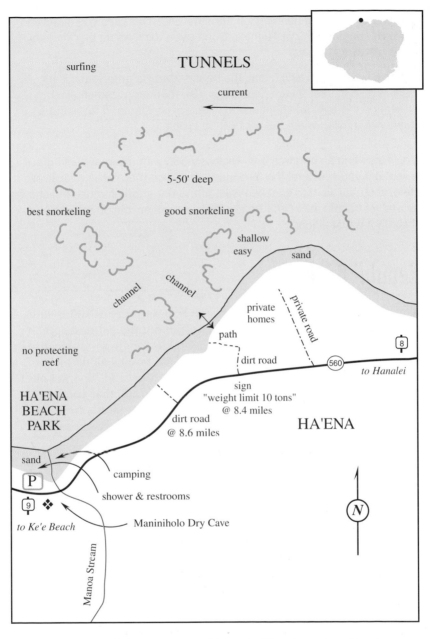

surfing

TUNNELS

current

5-50' deep

best snorkeling   good snorkeling

shallow
easy   sand

channel   channel

private
homes

path

dirt road

no protecting
reef

private road

560

to Hanalei

8

sign
"weight limit 10 tons"
@ 8.4 miles

**HA'ENA
BEACH
PARK**

dirt road
@ 8.6 miles

HA'ENA

sand

P

camping

9 ❖

shower & restrooms

to Ke'e Beach

Maniniholo Dry Cave

N

Manoa Stream

There are three public accesses to Tunnels. The closest parking is
found at the entrance at mile 8.4 where a short dirt road turns toward the
beach (the sign here says "Weight limit 10 tons"). Parking is allowed on
one side of the road only. A bit more parking is found on either side of
the highway, but all fills up quickly. Take this dirt road half a block to the

short palm-lined trail heading left from the end. This gets you directly to the best spot for entry at Tunnels. Don't even think about blocking anyone's driveway access.

Tunnels is a longish walk along the beach from Ha'ena Beach Park. Park at mile marker 9 (see map, page 49), then cross the shallow stream on the right and continue to hike across the sand for about a quarter of a mile, where the reef will be visible.

You'll also find a short trail from Highway 560 with minimal parking at mile 8.6 if you watch for the mile markers. Since there are no facilities here, you may want to continue west after your snorkel to use the shower and restrooms at Ha'ena Beach Park – another reason to simply park there in the first place.

Kepuhi Beach

This mile-long sand beach has a broad fringing reef offshore with alternating sandy channels and reef. While not the calmest spot, it can provide excellent snorkeling in favorable weather – especially in the summer. Access is blocked by the private homes along most of the beach, but Alamo'o Road will get you to the sand. Snorkel out to the reef, which is close to shore, watching carefully that you don't get caught in any current to the left. Large winter swells from the north will make it impossible, but there's a big reef area to explore when calm.

GETTING THERE Located to the ocean side of Highway 560, the beach is beyond private homes, so not very visible from the highway (see map, page 43). You will pass Wainiha Bay at mile marker 7, then Kepuhi Beach begins at the western point of Wainiha Bay and wraps around the corner toward the town of Ha'ena. Access is from Alamo'o or 'Ale'alea Roads, or by hiking from the highway or private homes. For the best snorkeling, head left (west) toward Tunnels.

Snuba

Snuba was developed as a simpler alternative to Scuba for shallow dives in resort conditions. Because Snuba divers are strictly limited in depth and conditions, and always accompanied by an instructor, training takes just 15-30 minutes. Two people share a small inflatable raft, which holds a Scuba air tank. A twenty-foot hose leads from the tank to a light harness on each diver. A soft, light weight belt completes your outfit. Very light and tropical!

Once in the water, your instructor teaches you to breathe through your regulator (which has a mouthpiece just like your snorkel) on the surface until you're completely comfortable. You're then free to swim around as you like – only down to twenty feet deep, of course. The raft will automatically follow you as you tour the bay.

It's that easy! You have to be at least eight years old, and have normal good health. Kids do amazingly well, and senior citizens can also enjoy Snuba.

We are certified Scuba divers, yet we tried Snuba because this was a perfect place to see what made it special. It actually has some advantages over Scuba in that you're free of the cumbersome equipment. There's none of the macho attitude you sometimes see on dive boats.

Snuba strikes us as a fun reasonably safe experience if you pay attention and use it according to directions. Where the reef is shallow, and conditions calm, it can actually be better than diving because you're so unencumbered in the water.

Warning: pay attention to the instructions because even at these shallow depths, you must know the proper way to surface. You must remember to never hold your breath as you ascend or you could force a bubble of air into your blood. Breathing out continually while surfacing is not intuitive, but absolutely necessary when you're breathing compressed air. This is especially important to remember if you're used to surface diving where you always hold your breath.

Enjoy and dive safely!

Wainiha Bay

This is a lovely, uncrowded beach with a large lagoon just to the west of Lumahai Beach. Since the Wainiha River flows in here, snorkeling isn't great. It's a nice place for a swim when calm. There's a wide sandy beach right near the highway and practically no people. Don't swim or snorkel here when north swell rolls in or heavy rain causes flooding. The Wainiha Valley drains from the beautiful 5,000 foot-high mountains in the background, so this river can rise quickly.

Snorkeling is best around the point to the left, and gets better as you head left into Kepuhi Beach.

GETTING THERE   Wainiha Bay can be seen from Highway 560 (see map, page 53). Parking is available in several spots along the road, and you'll have no crowds to worry about. Also no facilities. You'll find Wainiha just to the east of mile marker 7.

female bird wrasse

male bird wrasse

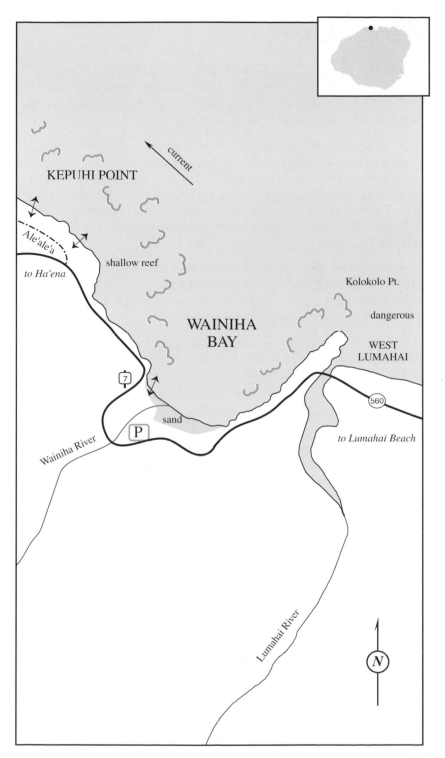

KEPUHI POINT

current

Ale'ale'a

to Ha'ena

shallow reef

Kolokolo Pt.

dangerous

WAINIHA
BAY

WEST
LUMAHAI

7

560

sand

P

to Lumahai Beach

Wainiha River

Lumahai River

N

Lumahai Beach

Lumahai is one of Kaua'i's most famous beaches and one of its loveliest. Scenes from the movie "South Pacific" were shot here in 1957 and Mount Makaha (close to Ke'e Beach) was inserted into the background to create the illusory Bali Hai.

You can catch a view of the picturesque eastern end of the beach from the highway at one of the turn-outs along Highway 56. To swim or snorkel, hike down a short, relatively easy path through the lush vegetation from the highway to get to this end of the beach. Parking is available at several locations along the highway, but the path itself is easy to miss in the dense foliage, so watch carefully for the mileage (see map, page 55) or you'll sail on by.

Lumahai is less protected than nearby beaches. Strong wave action often creates a steeply sloped beach with a wicked undertow. When conditions are poor, Lumahai still offers a delightful spot for a picnic and is well worth the short hike.

When calm enough, the swimming is excellent at the far right, while body-surfers play in the waves right in front. Snorkeling at Lumahai is fun, but you won't see much since there's no reef. Snorkel around the rocks watching for some of the local reef fish against dramatic rocks.

When big swells are rolling in (common in the winter), be extremely cautious. The undertow can be much worse than it looks and large sets of waves can arrive with no warning. Many have managed to drown themselves here (second only to Hanakapi'ai along the Na Pali coast). These statistics include people who were swept off the rocks and others caught in flash floods in the river. No lifeguards are on duty and no facilities are available at Lumahai.

While you will find a steep path to the western end of Lumahai (previously called Kahalahala for its hala trees), snorkeling or swimming anywhere except the eastern end is definitely too dangerous in any season.

GETTING THERE   Lumahai Beach is one of the easiest to miss. Watch the highway markers carefully (see map, page 55). There are several little turnouts along the highway, but note mile marker 4 as you drive up the hill leaving the Hanalei Valley. At exactly mile 4.75, you'll find the trail heading down to the beach. This easy trail is unmarked and can't be seen until you get out of the car. The trail, shaded by a lush canopy of lauhala trees, winds down to the east end of the beach. This section is your best bet for swimming or snorkeling.

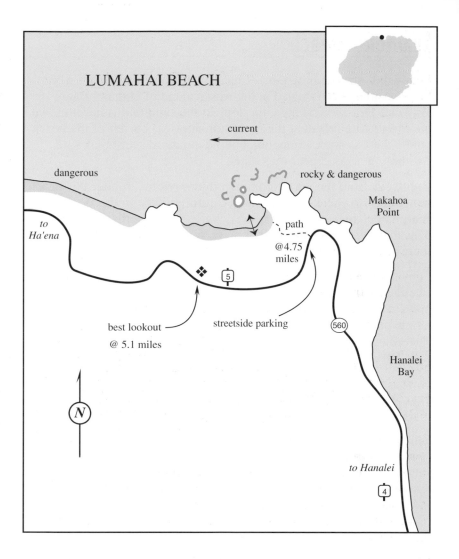

LUMAHAI BEACH

current

dangerous

rocky & dangerous

Makahoa
Point

to
Ha'ena

path

@4.75
miles

5

best lookout
@ 5.1 miles

streetside parking

560

Hanalei
Bay

N

to Hanalei

4

There is another trail further to the west, but the west section of Lumahai doesn't offer a safe spot to swim. Either trail can be slippery after heavy rains, which do happen suddenly and often in this green and lovely end of Kaua'i. Most showers here are warm and end in minutes, but heavy rain can settle in and cause flooding.

For the best overlook to take that picture of Lumahai, watch for mile marker 5 and then take the next turnout on the ocean (makai) side of the highway. This spot would be mile 5.1 although it isn't marked in any way. There are several other small turnouts, but only this one offers the classic view of Lumahai Beach.

Waikoko Beach

While this isn't the best snorkeling around, it's a lovely spot with broad sand beach. Located at the western end of Hanalei Bay, Waikoko Beach offers a gentle slope to the sand and is never crowded. Snorkeling is best at the far left (northwest) corner of the beach, where there is some protection behind a natural reef breakwater. Swimming is good near the center.

Big swells from the north (common in the winter) render this beach dangerous, so check out the waves carefully. Though the slope of the sand will change with the seasons, Waikoko is usually fairly shallow. This makes it better for snorkeling than swimming even though there's a sandy bottom. Heavy rains (common in northern Kaua'i) will bring brown-water runoff from the river.

GETTING THERE On the far western end of Hanalei Bay, you'll find this pretty and uncrowded beach along the highway. The beach can be seen as you pass the town of Hanalei heading west (see map, page 57). There's a parking area on the makai side of the highway near mile marker 4. There are no facilities at this end of Hanalei Bay.

Wai'oli Beach Park (Pine Trees)

This beach with restrooms and showers is located toward the center of Hanalei Bay. The lovely trees shading this beach are actually ironwoods. Snorkeling is poor, but swimming is OK except during periods of high north swell in the winter. When calm, the water is nearly flat with a wide sandy beach great for little kids – especially in the summer. Winter swells can sweep right through, making it unavailable for either swimming or snorkeling.

Wai'oli Beach Park is on Weke Road (the road that follow the edge of Hanalei Bay.) Either He'e Road or 'Ama'ama Road will take you to Weke Road from Highway 560. This is near the center of Hanalei Bay only blocks from the town of Hanalei, so it can be reached quickly for a shower after snorkeling in a more isolated location. The name Hanalei means lei-shaped bay, so Wai'oli is the middle of the lei. Heavy rains make this beach too murky for snorkeling.

GETTING THERE Wai'oli Beach Park is just two blocks from the town of Hanalei (where you will see mile marker 3), but is well-hidden from the highway. Turn toward the bay on any street from the center of town and you'll find the park at the center of Hanalei Bay. It's located on Weke Road (see map, page 57). There's plenty of parking and all facilities.

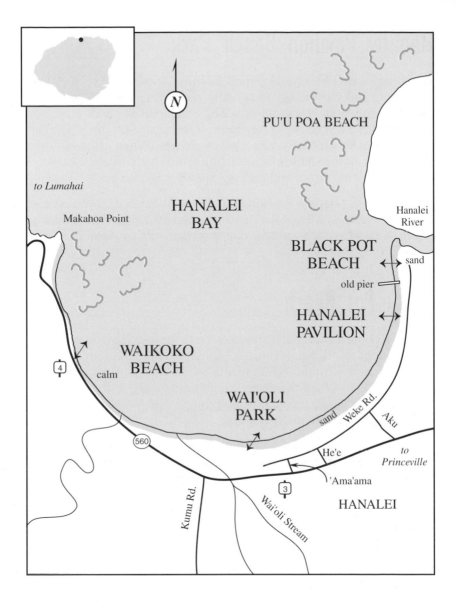

to Lumahai

Makahoa Point

HANALEI
BAY

PU'U POA BEACH

Hanalei
River

BLACK POT
BEACH

sand

old pier

HANALEI
PAVILION

WAIKOKO
BEACH

calm

WAI'OLI
PARK

sand

Weke Rd.

Aku

He'e

to
Princeville

'Ama'ama

HANALEI

Kumu Rd.

Wai'oli Stream

trumpetfish

Hanalei Pavilion Beach Park

While you'll find lifeguards and all facilities available here, the swimming and snorkeling aren't really great – especially when winter swells roll straight into the bay. The Hanalei River adds fresh water nearby, so visibility is low most of the year. Still, it's a popular spot and can be very calm when waves are low. When calm, children play happily in the shallow water lapping the sandy beach. Showers, restrooms, picnic tables and parking are all available here.

GETTING THERE   Hanalei Pavilion is another park located on Weke Road (between Wai'oli and Black Pot Beaches). See map, page 57. Just take any road from the city toward the bay, then turn right on Weke Road and you will come to the pavilion.

Black Pot Beach

This is a popular beach that stretches from the old Hanalei pier to the mouth of the Hanalei River. When calm, children enjoy the wide sand and shallow water. When winter swells roll in, this can be a dangerous spot. When that happens, sit on the sand and enjoy the gorgeous view of the mountains towering over the west end of the valley with waterfalls in abundance.

All facilities, including camping, showers, restrooms, picnic tables, boat launch and plenty of parking are available here. There's lots of sand, but the beach is all fairly shallow. Since the Hanalei River pours into the bay here, visibility will be poor most of the time, making it better for splashing than snorkeling.

Dedicated snorkelers may want to cross the river and snorkel near Pu'u Poa Beaches. While it's a long swim, you might prefer the swim to climbing Pu'u Poa's 171 steps. Also, there are lots more parking spaces at Black Pot Beach.

GETTING THERE   Black Pot is the beach at the far east of Hanalei Bay where the Hanalei River enters the bay (see map, page 57). It's located at the far northeastern end of Weke Road and hard to miss. You'll find ample parking and all facilities here. From Highway 560, just turn toward the ocean anywhere in the town of Hanalei, then right on Weke Road to the end.

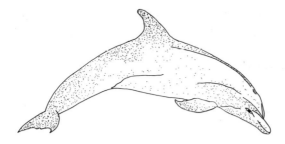

bottlenose dolphin

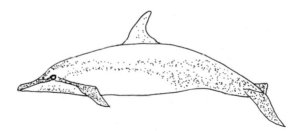

spinner dolphin

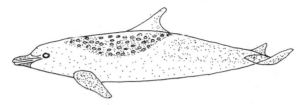

spotted dolphin

Princeville Area

Princeville, a planned community located on a bluff overlooking the north coast of Kaua'i, is packed with hotels, condos, timeshares, restaurants, and homes. You'll find a golf course, supermarket, public library, and shopping, all in the center of Princeville, near the main entrance from Highway 56 at Ka Haku Road.

Beaches here are all found down about two hundred feet below a steep bluff. Views are outstanding up on top, but snorkeling requires a hike. Some of the paths are relatively easy, while others require a difficult, and sometimes slippery and treacherous, scramble down the cliff. Because of the climb, most Princeville beaches are uncrowded and you may have them all to yourself.

Snorkeling, as well as swimming, can range from very easy in flat water to impossible when huge winter swells arrive from the north. Heavy rains can sometimes make most of the trails impassable. Still, when conditions are good (more often in the summer), these beaches are beautiful and mostly secluded. An offshore reef wraps much, but not all, of this northern area. Turtles abound along the cliffs and you may even see baby turtles in the natural salt-water swimming pool called Queen Emma's Bath.

If you're not staying in Princeville itself, parking is a serious problem. It's hard to understand why Princeville has chosen to provide so little visitor parking – since most of the folks parking to enjoy these beaches probably are staying elsewhere in Princeville. They penalize all of their guests in order to exclude a few visitors. We hope they'll adjust their attitude about this. But for the time being, come very early if you want the best chance to park and enjoy the many little Princeville beaches. When the few ten-car public parking lots fill, all the other available parking lots are private and sport prominent tow-away signs, though we doubt that they're quick to tow.

Princeville is green and gorgeous in the winter when hundreds of waterfalls cascade into Hanalei Valley. Summer usually provides the calmest water for water sports here. At times in the summer, the north can even be calmer than Po'ipu, because summer swells arrive from the south. We've listed the Princeville snorkeling sites in clockwise order as we follow the coast around Kaua'i.

Pause while you snorkel, float easy and soak in the gorgeous views looking out to sea and back toward the mountains beyond the Hanalei Valley. You'll be glad you made the effort to discover Princeville's secluded coves.

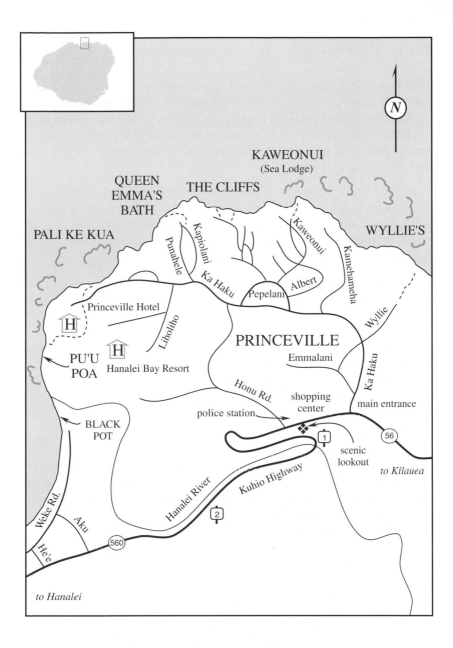

KAWEONUI
(Sea Lodge)

QUEEN
EMMA'S
BATH

THE CLIFFS

WYLLIE'S

PALI KE KUA

Kapiolani

Kaweonui

Punahele

Ka Haku

Kamehameha

Pepelani

Albert

Princeville Hotel

Liholiho

PRINCEVILLE

Wyllie

PU'U
POA

Hanalei Bay Resort

Emmalani

Ka Haku

Honu Rd.

shopping
center

main entrance

police station

BLACK
POT

scenic
lookout

56

to Kilauea

Hanalei River

Kuhio Highway

Weke Rd.

Aku

He'e

560

to Hanalei

N

H

H

1

2

needlefish

Pu'u Poa Beach (at the Princeville Hotel)

Pu'u Poa's two beaches are located down below the Princeville Hotel (only 171 concrete steps). Since all of the Princeville beaches are about two hundred feet down from the bluff, you'll need to hike to get to the water, so the choice is steps, slippery path, ramp or dangerous path. Pu'u Poa and Wyllie's are the easiest – steps at Pu'u Poa and a ramping path at Wyllie's.

While Hanalei Bay can be closed out with huge breakers when north swell rolls in, it can also be completely calm in the summer. At that time, it's possible to snorkel out from Pu'u Poa in 5-10 feet of water, then to the north and around the bend to several little isolated beaches. In some ways this is a better beach for snorkeling than swimming: there are reef and boulders almost everywhere. This extensive fringing reef offers protection only when the big surfing waves stay away. Summer is far more likely to be calm.

While this isn't the best snorkeling beach in northern Kaua'i, and isn't usually very clear, there's still enough to see if you take the time and wander. Once we happened upon a couple of white-tipped reef sharks close to shore in about ten feet of water. You won't see great coral here or a lot of fish, but you're almost certain to see turtles if you stay out for awhile. They're abundant along the cliffs as you snorkel along the coast to the north. When swells permit, stop to visit one of the tiny isolated sandy coves along the base of the cliff.

The well-hidden public path to Pu'u Poa Beach begins just to the left of the gatehouse as you approach the Princeville Hotel (see map, page 63). A ten-car parking lot makai (toward the ocean) from the path provides parking for both Pu'u Poa and Pali Ke Kua.

When you get down to the beach, you can scramble over some rocks on the left to get to a nearly-empty second beach. This is easiest when the tide is low. Snorkelers, however, will probably prefer to enter from the main beach since the best snorkeling is to the right (north). Entry is easy here from the sand, but it pays to watch for rocks. When winter swells hit hard, you won't want to get in the water for either swimming or snorkeling. Ask at the Princeville water sports office (at the north end of the beach) if in doubt.

GETTING THERE   From Highway 56, take the main Princeville entrance, which is Ka Haku Road. The public access parking lot is found on the right just before you get to the Princeville Hotel parking (see map, page 63). This small lot holds ten cars at best and serves two beaches. There's little legal parking available anywhere else in the area.

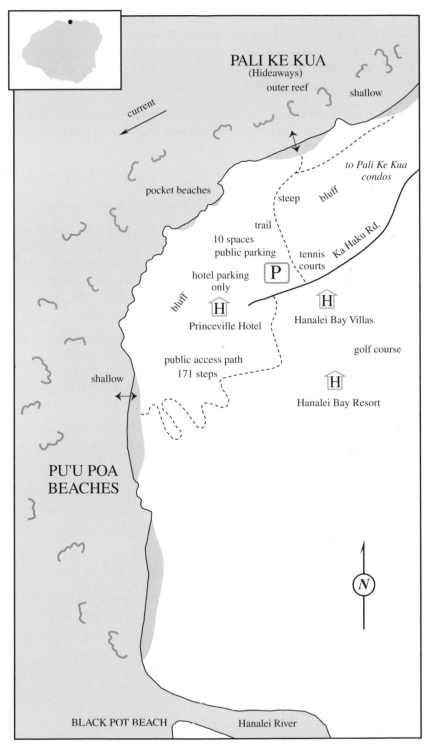

PALI KE KUA
(Hideaways)

outer reef

shallow

current

to Pali Ke Kua
condos

pocket beaches

steep   bluff

trail

Ka Haku Rd.

10 spaces
public parking

P

tennis
courts

hotel parking
only

H

Princeville Hotel

bluff

H

Hanalei Bay Villas

golf course

public access path
171 steps

shallow

H

Hanalei Bay Resort

PU'U POA
BEACHES

N

BLACK POT BEACH   Hanalei River

63

Across the street from this parking lot, you'll find the trail heading off toward the golf course. Follow the trail until it winds back to the right toward the Princeville Hotel. You'll pass their pool and eventually arrive at the beach. There are two beaches here, but the best entry for snorkeling is just to the right of where the path emerges on the sand.

When the public parking fills, some people park along the service road at the south of the hotel and walk down that way. However, it's possible this would get you towed.

Pali Ke Kua Beach (Hideaways)

These two secluded beaches are also called Hideaways or, less often, Kenomeme. Located between the Princeville Hotel and the Pali Ke Kua condos, the Pali Ke Kua beaches offer snorkeling when conditions are relatively calm – especially in the summer. They have broad shallow areas near shore, making both beaches poor swimming destinations. In fact, even snorkeling is best at high tide.

Access requires hiking down about two hundred feet from the road from two separate locations. Once down to the beach, you can snorkel from one to the other IF calm enough that swells won't slap you against the coral or rocks. When very calm, advanced snorkelers can roam outside the fringing reef.

Snorkeling is good if conditions are favorable. The best snorkeling is at the far right end in a tiny protected area tucked into the eastern point. Access to this protected area is best from the condos on a path marked private and well-hidden just within the Pali Ke Kua condo area. The snorkeling at the end of this ramped path is calmer, deeper and a bit more clear. While the path is easy, you will have to scramble over a rocky area to get to the far right.

For public access, you must snorkel or hike from the beach at the western end, where there are only ten designated parking spaces at the start of the trail – with no other legal parking nearby. The hike is fairly difficult over rocks and the swim is over some shallow reef. All in all, access to Pali Ke Kua is challenging unless you happen to be staying at the conveniently located condos.

Most of the Pali Ke Kua reef area has poor visibility when swells roll in from the north, but we did see huge schools of tangs (many hundreds) grazing along the reef. Most of the reef is 5-20' deep. The reef further offshore has lots of turtles, but the poor visibility can make them difficult to see. Visibility and fun greatly improve here when seas are extra calm.

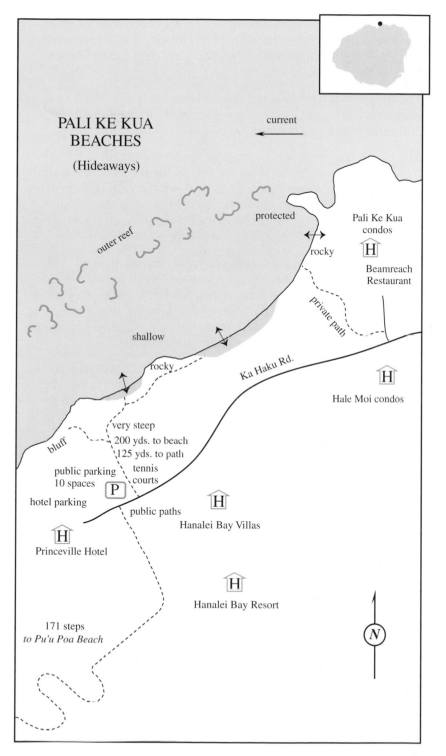

PALI KE KUA
BEACHES

(Hideaways)

current

Pali Ke Kua
condos

protected

outer reef

rocky

Beamreach
Restaurant

private path

shallow

rocky

Ka Haku Rd.

Hale Moi condos

very steep
200 yds. to beach
125 yds. to path

bluff

public parking
10 spaces

tennis
courts

P

hotel parking

public paths

Hanalei Bay Villas

Princeville Hotel

Hanalei Bay Resort

171 steps
to Pu'u Poa Beach

N

If not so calm, you can still enjoy the lovely beach with its false kamani trees (the ones with edible nuts looking like Brazil nuts) and hala trees that appear to be standing on stilts (one of world's most ancient trees).

The trail to Pali Ke Kua is best when completely dry. You'll need to walk about 125 yards to the edge of the bluff, then descend about 200 yards to the beach below.

The hike takes you down steep steps with a guard railing for the first half, then a steep slope for the rest of the way. There is a rope available to help assure you don't slide down the path. This is definitely not the place to go after a heavy rain because the soil in Kaua'i gets slippery very fast. The trail is too difficult for small children or anyone who isn't strong and steady.

Notice that all of our maps are arranged so that north is up. This will help you decide where to go when swells roll in from storms across the Pacific. Pali Ke Kua catches the full north swell, except for the little semi-protected corner at the far right. While the outer reef here offers some protection from waves, it isn't enough to keep the biggest waves from washing all the way to shore.

GETTING THERE   From Highway 56, take the major Princeville entrance (Ka Haku Road) toward the ocean. Curve along Ka Haku to the northwest and eventually you'll come to the "guard" station just before the Princeville Hotel. Park here on your right in a small marked public parking lot that holds about ten cars at best. The small sign here says "public access to beach."

This one small public lot serves Pali Ke Kua as well as Pu'u Poa, and there's virtually no alternative parking available, so come very early to find a space (certainly before 9 a.m.). The public trail to Pali Ke Kua heads toward the ocean (while the trail across the street heads toward Pu'u Poa). You'll need to walk the narrow path between the parking lot and the Pu'u Poa tennis courts, then pass the pool, for about 125 yards to get to the trail at the edge of the bluff (see map, page 65). Here you'll find steps with a railing for the first half, then a security rope for the next half. This trail (about 200 yards) is way too slippery after a heavy rain and requires caution at all times because it's very steep.

After reaching the beach, you may want to continue to the section further to the right. If so, you'll have to climb over boulders that separate these two beaches.

If you happen to be staying in the Pali Ke Kua condos (the Beamreach Restaurant turnoff), there's a asphalt path available just inside the condo entrance that is fairly steep, but much safer. Signs here warn "private" and "towaway zone."

The best snorkeling is found at this eastern end of the beaches, but still requires a scramble over some rocks to the right. The reef near shore is quite shallow, especially at low tide. Off to the right is a pretty little area that is somewhat protected by the point curving in at the far right. The water here is about 5-20' deep and can be clearer than the rest of the beach.

There are no facilities near Pali Ke Kua. Just sand and shade. From the ocean side of Ka Haku Road, you can get a good view of the beaches.

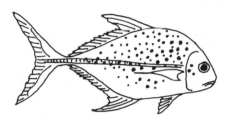

bluefin trevally jack

One of our sentimental favorites. While requiring a hike down about two hundred feet from the Princeville plateau at the end of Punahele Road, this natural saltwater swimming pool (complete with fish) is well worth the effort. Check our map (page 69) because it's hard to find. Don't be discouraged too soon because you won't see it until you round a corner and voila! At this time parking is limited to about ten marked spaces, so come early (certainly before 9 a.m.) to find parking. Besides, you may have the enchanting pool to yourselves! High surf may make the pool unsafe in the winter, but small waves at low tide simply splash into the north and west side of the pool, swirling in and filling the water with bubbles like a hot tub.

After hiking down the path and past the waterfall, then over the smooth (pahoehoe) lava rocks to the left, you'll pass several smaller pools and tiny coves, eventually arriving at the lava-walled pool about the size of a home swimming pool. When waves aren't huge, the lava protects the pool from all but a fun splash and a gentle waterfall at the north end. This is a delightful spot you won't want to miss. At five to ten feet deep, it's fine for swimming, but even better for snorkeling, because you can see better and avoid kicking rocks with your bare feet.

We saw hundreds of fish in the pool – including close-up views of colorful Christmas wrasses, raccoon butterflyfish, saddle wrasses, sergeant majors, and unusual blennies. We hear that baby turtles are sometimes seen in the pool. No need for fins here, so don't bother to bring them. Of course, there are no facilities of any kind down at Queen Emma's Bath – not even sand. Only the natural bubble bath.

This is a unique and beautiful spot. Besides snorkeling and swimming, you can look out across the Hanalei Valley to the dramatic mountains in the distance. Incoming salt water forms a waterfall at the north end of the pool, while waves sometimes splash into the middle filling the pool with bubbles. Low tide will be the quietest time to snorkel here. When waves are high enough (especially winter swells), it can be dangerous.

Treat this area with respect. This isn't the place for cannonballing into the pool. You'll never find a pool with a spectacular backdrop quite like this..

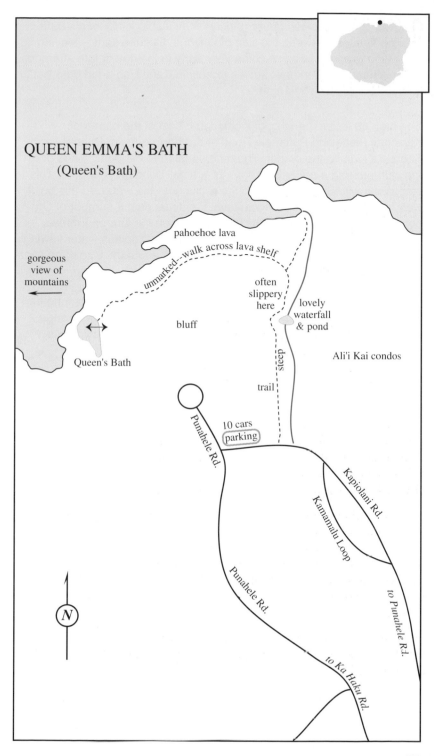

QUEEN EMMA'S BATH
(Queen's Bath)

pahoehoe lava

unmarked--walk across lava shelf

gorgeous
view of
mountains

often
slippery
here

lovely
waterfall
& pond

bluff

Queen's Bath

Ali'i Kai condos

steep

trail

Punahele Rd.

10 cars
parking

Kapiolani Rd.

Kamamalu Loop

to Punahele Rd.

Punahele Rd.

to Ka Haku Rd.

N

GETTING THERE Limited public parking is available for Queen's Bath. The ten spaces (between the little blue signs) fill quite early – leaving no other legal place to park, so come very early in the day or late afternoon. Keep in mind that darkness settles rapidly in Kaua'i, so head back out in time to hike while it's still light.

See map 69 for the parking lot located just east of the corner of Kapiolani Place and Punahele Road at the north edge of Princeville. There's a sign on the corner. The path, located to the right, winds down the bluff passing a pretty waterfall into a small pond on your right. This steep path will lead eventually to the rocks near the water. At this point, walk left on fairly flat and smooth lava. Continue past a number of tiny pools and a couple of bays until you come upon the Queen Emma's Bath, which will be completely enclosed with wave splash water flowing in at the far north and out at the southwest. It's about the size of an average backyard pool.

This is more or less the end of the hike, so you can't miss it as long as you go far enough. You'll be able to look back at the mountain range beyond Hanalei Valley from the Queen's Bath – something you won't see until you reach this point.

The Cliffs

If staying in Princeville and you happen to find the ocean perfectly calm, you might be tempted to try the path down the cliff at the far north. There's no beach here and the cliff is steep. Besides, entry is from the lava rocks. This is definitely not for a beginner, but the water can be clear and turtles abundant. We've seen it calm as bathwater, which is what you need to enter the water from rocks in the north. Advanced snorkelers only due to changeable conditions, which could make your exit challenging. From the top of the bluff, you're likely to see turtles grazing along the rocks – especially in the late afternoon when winds die down.

GETTING THERE It's best to be staying at or near the Cliff's Resort in Princeville, since no public parking is provided. The trail down from their property is marked at the edge of the bluff with a discouraging sign. It is steep and can be dangerous when slippery. Take great care when entering the water from lava and watch that swells aren't picking up. Snorkel along the cliff in either direction watching carefully to find your exit later. Leave something bright to mark the spot where you enter the water because this isn't the place to get lost.

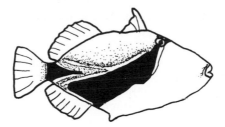

rectangular triggerfish

Picasso triggerfish

71

Kaweonui Beach (Sea Lodge Beach)

Kaweonui (also called Sea Lodge Beach, after the name of the condo just up the bluff) is difficult to find and offers no public parking, but this is one of our favorites. Even guests at Princeville may have a hard time finding the way. You can check our map (page 73) for the location of the trail that heads from the north Princeville cliff about two hundred feet down to the beach. The jungle trail itself is beautiful under lush false kamani, hala and other tropical trees with birds singing in the treetops.

The path is narrow, but maintained. There are some fairly steep spots, so avoid this trail after a heavy rain, which would make the path quite dangerously slippery. Go slow and enjoy the beauty of this trail and the smell of wild guava that abound. At the bottom, you will need to hike to the left over some rocks, but not for far – only about one hundred feet.

The small beach has coarse sand and deep shade and is usually empty. The inner bay is too shallow for swimming, but excellent for snorkeling when swell is low. Winter often brings big waves from the north and low tide will provide poor clearance, so choose your time carefully. Tides in Hawai'i only vary by about two feet, but at Kaweonui that means the difference between one-foot clearance and three as you skim the reef to the outer wall. While the inner area is fairly protected by outer reef, don't take chances in a shallow site like this if there's any possibility of larger sets that could mash you on the rocks or coral. Even the sand beach is unsafe in severe winter storms.

We enter on the right side of the beach (see map, page 73) in a small channel that angles to the right out of the shallowest area. Then snorkel left across the shallow reef to explore the outer edge where the water is six to twenty feet deep – perfect for snorkeling. Wandering over the shallow reef, we saw a large octopus at close range just feet from the sand. Larger fish were darting about in the crevices (about five feet below the reef's surface). Outside the edge of the reef, parrotfish, turtles, and pelagic fish were everywhere in about twenty feet of water.

GETTING THERE Kaweonui (commonly called Sea Lodge Beach for the condos up on top) has no public parking and can be difficult to find. You can park elsewhere and walk in from wherever you find parking, or stay in one of Princeville's many condos and walk to the start of the trail.

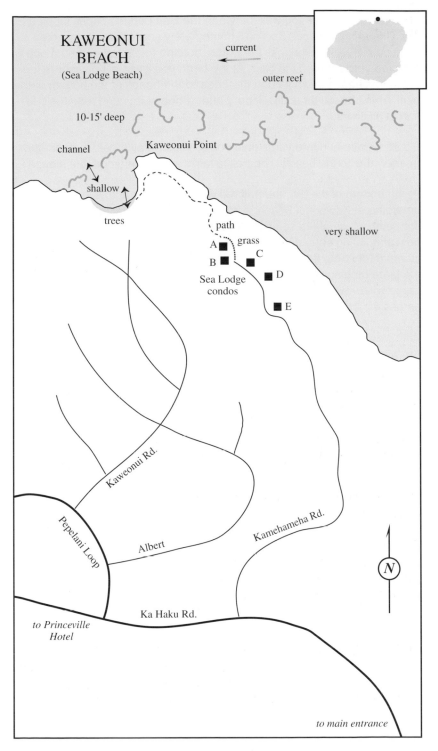

KAWEONUI
BEACH
(Sea Lodge Beach)

current

outer reef

10-15' deep

channel

Kaweonui Point

shallow

trees

path

grass

very shallow

A

B

C

D

E

Sea Lodge
condos

Kaweonui Rd.

Pepelani Loop

Albert

Kamehameha Rd.

N

Ka Haku Rd.

to Princeville
Hotel

to main entrance

The path starts after you walk between the Sea Lodge condos labeled B and C (see map, page 73). You'll immediately come to a sign marked "section A". Walk out across the grass, holding to the left for about one hundred yards toward the bluff. At the bluff, you'll see a sign, where the steep trail heads down though the trees to the beach at the bottom of the bluff. This trail will be quite slippery after a heavy rain and requires caution at all times.

Go about one hundred yards until you cross a small creek, then another quarter mile to the beach. The trail is fairly well-maintained, but steep.

At the bottom of the cliff, the trail will wind to the left across a rocky area, emerging at Kaweonui Beach, a small sand beach tucked to the left of the point, which offers some protection from surf. Check our map for the best snorkeling entry point at the right, where you will find a narrow channel (of sorts) through the reef. This will get you to the far edge of the large fringing reef running all the way to and across 'Anini Beach. Large winter waves can sweep across this protecting reef all the way across the beach, so stay away in bad weather.

With calm weather and a high tide, it's a delightful spot. Follow the narrow sandy "channel" that angles to the right (see map, page 73), then take a left turn when you have enough clearance and cross over the reef to the outer edge. Snorkel in either direction along the far edge of the reef, but do remember to note the channel location in order to return to the same spot for exit.

Low tide won't provide quite enough clearance at the entry point, so be sure to check the tide tables if you want to snorkel at Kaweonui Beach. Bring your wetsuit too if you have one. Beginners may find the reef here too claustrophobic, but experienced snorkelers will love it.

juvenile yellowtail coris

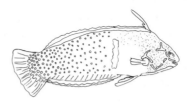

adult yellowtail coris

juvenile rockmover wrasse

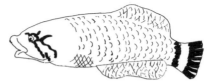

adult rockmover wrasse

Wyllie's Beach   (Puamana)

Wyllie's Beach, at the far eastern end of Princeville, requires a fairly easy quarter-mile hike down the overgrown remnants of an old ranch road flanked by two rows of canopy trees. No stairs are required here, but the trail ramps enough to be slippery after a heavy rain. It's a pleasant walk even if you don't plan to get in the water.

The trail is well-hidden. Although there is no designated parking, it's easy to find a spot along the side of the road. Just avoid parking in any of the condo lots, where you risk being towed. The access may change when the big empty field sprouts condos one day.

We weren't impressed with the snorkeling, but it's a beautiful small beach, completely empty, and quite calm as long as huge swells aren't rolling in from the north. High tide is essential if you plan to snorkel here and want any clearance between your body and the coral. It's all too shallow for swimming. This broad flat expanse of coral is located just to the west of the 'Anini River. Stay well to the left to avoid any current near the river. Snorkel anywhere within the shallow area. There isn't a lot to see, but you might just spot an octopus. You'll sometimes see locals hunting here with spear guns when the tide is high and surf is low, so don't be surprised to see the octopuses do their best to disguise themselves – and their best is VERY good because they can change both color and texture.

Most of the surf will break far out along the outer edge of the reef, but higher breakers bring stronger currents pulling toward the left and out of the channels – particularly the river channel.

GETTING THERE   Located in the northeast corner of Princeville, this path is unmarked. From Highway 56 as you enter Princeville, take Ka Haku Road (see map, page 77) and turn right (toward the ocean) on Wyllie. You'll see the Paniolo condos on the right-hand corner. Go to the end of Wyllie and park along the road near this turn-around, where you'll see the Puamano condos on your left.

From the turnaround, walk toward the water across the grassy field toward the bluff. After about 100 yards, duck right through the line of trees along the edge of the golf course and you'll find the old road ramping down to the water – about a quarter of a mile away. It's just one long gradual slope, and doesn't require any dangerous rock hopping or stairs. You can't miss the beach at the end of the trail. When snorkeling or swimming, stay left, away from the 'Anini River channel, especially when winter swells make the river channel current dangerous.

76

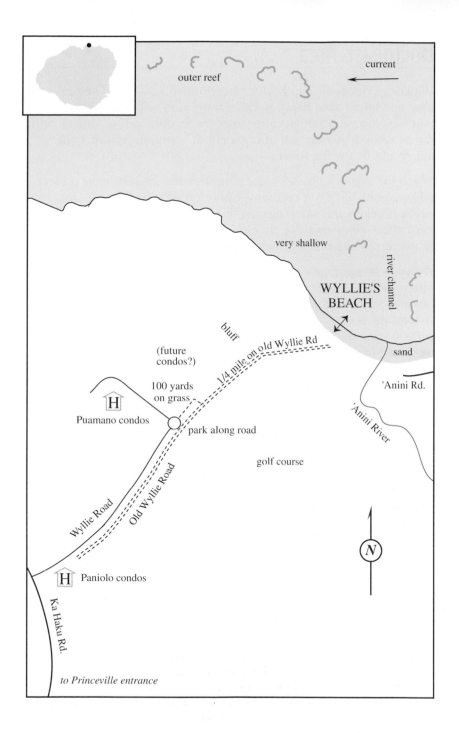

current

outer reef

very shallow

WYLLIE'S
BEACH

river channel

bluff

(future
condos?)

1/4 mile on old Wyllie Rd

sand

'Anini Rd.

100 yards
on grass

H

Puamano condos

park along road

'Anini River

golf course

Wyllie Road

Old Wyllie Road

N

H Paniolo condos

Ka Haku Rd.

to Princeville entrance

Northeast Area

Between Princeville and Kilauea Lighthouse, you'll find several very long and broad sand beaches. Conditions vary with the weather, so you can't always count on calm water (especially in the winter). Still, the beaches are lovely and offer plenty of room to explore, both above and below the water.

When the tide is high, 'Anini Beach offers the longest inner protected lagoon in Kaua'i. A reef far offshore protects the lagoon from the heavy breakers that crash against this reef most of the year. A beach park offers all amenities right along the water with plenty of space to wander in either direction within the inner lagoon.

Kauapea Beach requires a moderate hike down into a ravine, but offers an excellent and secluded mile-long beach, although no facilities are available here. While often too rough for safe snorkeling or swimming, it's still worth a visit. Kalihiwai Bay can be reached by car and offers a bit more protection from swells. Kilauea Bay requires the longest hike and catches the eastern swells.

With no hotels or condos in this less-developed northeast area, accommodations are found entirely in private homes. Many are found along 'Anini Road right near the water. Look for the rental signs out in front.

The big beaches of the northeast are also popular for other water sports, such as windsurfing, surfing, kayaking, fishing, and the latest craze, kitesurfing.

spotted boxfish

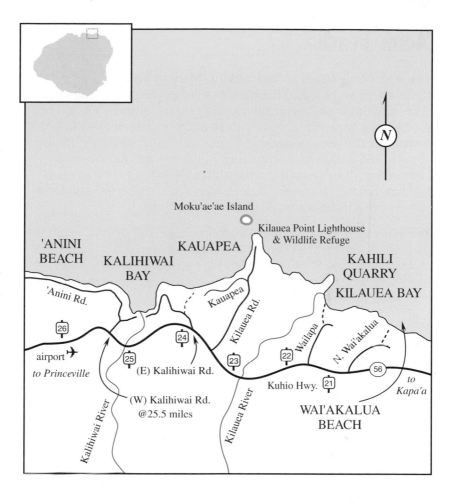

'ANINI
BEACH

KALIHIWAI
BAY

KAUAPEA

Moku'ae'ae Island

Kilauea Point Lighthouse
& Wildlife Refuge

KAHILI
QUARRY

KILAUEA BAY

'Anini Rd.

Kauapea

Kilauea Rd.

Wailapa

N. Wai'akalua

26

airport ✈

to Princeville

25

24

23

22

56

to
Kapa'a

(E) Kalihiwai Rd.

Kuhio Hwy. 21

(W) Kalihiwai Rd.
@25.5 miles

Kalihiwai River

Kilauea River

WAI'AKALUA
BEACH

N

saddleback butterflyfish

'Anini Beach

This miles-long beach (called Wanini, Manini, Kalihiwai, or even Kalihikai on some maps) has plenty of room to explore. The tide-pools and tiny coves at the far east offer private little beaches. The center has a large public park with showers, restrooms, picnic tables, barbeques, camping, grass, boat launch, and ample parking. It's a popular destination for windsurfing, kayaking, and more recently kite-surfing. 'Anini Beach is almost entirely protected by an outer reef that catches the waves. Many beach access paths are also located between private homes that front 'Anini Road.

The inner area where you can snorkel is huge, but shallow and not particularly interesting. The coral is largely covered with brown algae, so you have to swim awhile to see much. There are some spots with a bit of coral and fish, but mostly out toward the reef edge or along any of the channels.

When the sea is calm and tide is high, snorkeling here is easy with a distinct drift to the left. Our preference is to enter the water to the right (see map, page 81) and drift along through a couple of miles of shallow reef (checking out channels along the way), then hike back to the car. Somewhere along the line you're likely to spot turtles in deeper channels and an octopus in the shallows. While most of the inner reef is shallow (1-5 feet), the channels drop off to as much as forty feet deep as they approach the outer barrier reef.

When heavy swells hit northern Kaua'i in the winter, 'Anini may still look wonderfully calm. However, all the water that pours over that far outer reef has to find its way back eventually. This means the channels can pull you out with the water. Take a good look at those distant waves and remind yourself that you'd rather not snorkel IN them. Stay away from any channel that tugs outward. This goes double for the 'Anini River at the far western end of the beach.

Give 'Anini Beach a try in calm conditions with high tide and enjoy watching the kite-surfing (especially around 3-4 p.m. when the winds are up). Shower, hang out at the park, and enjoy this long lovely beach. Just don't expect large numbers of fish or coral.

GETTING THERE The west section of Kalihiwai Road exits Highway 56 at mile 25.5 (see map, page 81). This end of the road, which is 2.5 miles east of the Princeville entrance, is no longer connected to the south end of Kalihiwai Road since a tsunami took out the bridge years ago. Head toward the water on Kalihiwai Road for .2 of a mile, then take the Y to the left, which will be 'Anini Road. In less than a mile, this road will follow

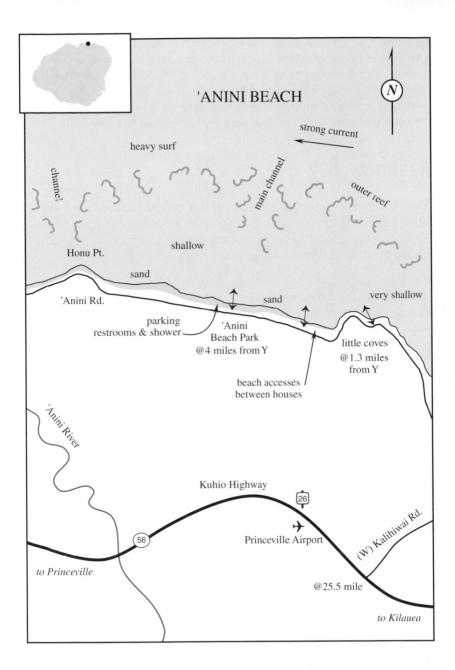

'ANINI BEACH

strong current

heavy surf

channel

main channel

outer reef

Honu Pt.

shallow

sand

'Anini Rd.

sand

very shallow

parking
restrooms & shower

'Anini
Beach Park
@4 miles from Y

little coves
@1.3 miles
from Y

beach accesses
between houses

'Anini River

Kuhio Highway

26

56

Princeville Airport

(W) Kalihiwai Rd.

to Princeville

@25.5 mile

to Kilauea

the beach to the end at the 'Anini River. In the middle of this two-mile
long beach (four miles from the start of 'Anini Road), you'll find the beach
park with all facilities: shower, restrooms, covered picnic tables, small
boat ramp and camping. Inland, across the street (mauka) is the Kaua'i
Polo Club.

As you leave Kalihiwai Road, the first stretch of 'Anini Road offers many lovely small pools, great for a quiet picnic or some wading. You may wish to enter the water here to have a gliding snorkel along the inshore reef, but will usually have to hike back to your car due to the slow, but relentless, current that heads west. You may want to bring along some flip-flops on your snorkel to save your feet from the hot pavement.

Kalihiwai Bay

This broad sand beach in a protected bay can be reached from two sides, but the river separates the two sections (see map, page 83). Kalihiwai Road used to be connected, but a tsunami washed out the bridge over the Kalihiwai River.

For river access, camping and kayaking, the west end is good with shade under the ironwoods along a river deep enough for kayaking. Snorkelers and swimmers, however, will prefer to access Kalihiwai Bay from the east.

The eastern side of Kalihiwai Valley offers a relatively calm bay with wide sand beach, river to the left, and cliffs along the far right, where the bay is usually calmest.

When calm, this is an excellent swimming beach with some snorkeling along the cliffs. The middle is all sand. This is a popular family spot for picnics and boogie-boarding. Kayaking up the river is very popular, although signs warn of leptospirosis danger (see page 109), so be aware of this risk if boating or swimming in the fresh water.

Kalihiwai Bay is deep, well-protected and very pretty, although there are no public facilities in the area.

GETTING THERE Since the west and east sections of Kalihiwai Road are no longer connected, there are two ways to reach this beach. The western section of Kalihiwai Road (1.5 miles northwest at mile 25.5) gets you to the sand and the river, but not to the best snorkeling. For kayaking, follow this road to the end about half a mile down to the river.

For snorkeling and swimming, it's best to take the eastern section of Kalihiwai Road (1.5 miles southeast) toward the water. This section of Kalihiwai Road (just east of mile marker 24) will wind along the bluff toward the north. Stay left at the Y and eventually double back southwest to drop down to the bay. You'll find plenty of parking here under the ironwoods along a broad sandy beach. While swimming and body-boarding are good in the middle of the bay, snorkeling is better at the far right along the cliff(see map, page 83).

82

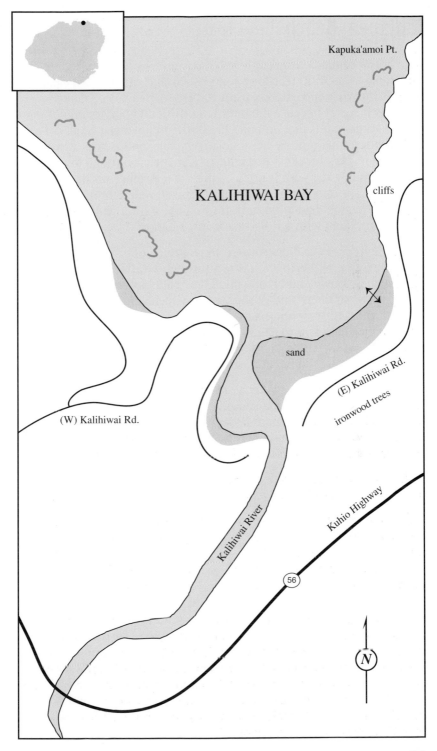

Kapuka'amoi Pt.

KALIHIWAI BAY

cliffs

sand

(E) Kalihiwai Rd.

ironwood trees

(W) Kalihiwai Rd.

Kalihiwai River

Kuhio Highway

56

N

Kauapea Beach (Secret Beach)

One of our romantic tropical beach favorites. Secret Beach seems an odd name for a 3,000 feet-long sand beach that can be seen clearly from Princeville and extends from Kalihiwai Beach to Kilauea Point. Is it secret because the path is so difficult? No, it's one of the easiest access paths that descend the bluffs in northern Kaua'i. The hike down through the ravine is relatively safe, and is well worth the effort even if big breakers often make Kauapea too rough to snorkel or swim. While the path is not as dangerous as other north shore hikes, a heavy rain can make the muddy path much more challenging. The "Secret" had to do with finding the trail down, which is no longer a problem with a little inside information.

This is a gorgeous and uncrowded long stretch of caramel-colored sand. The hike will bring you down through a valley of tropical trees such as kiawe and breadfruit. The public access path drops you down on the southern end of the beach, which is not usually the best place to snorkel. It is, however, a great place to walk on the beach, wade in the shallow protected ponds at the south end of the sand, and check out the cliffs with unusual basalt columns and caves with fresh water pools. When calm, strong swimmers can snorkel to the left along the lava.

The beach changes with the seasons, but often offers very protected pools of shallow water where little kids can have a great time, at the far south end of the beach where sand meets lava. In heavy surf, be extremely careful when climbing on the lava because a sudden swell can sweep you into the ocean. The big winter storms take away huge amounts of sand, so the beach that stretches for a mile in summer can become three small beaches late in the winter.

When calm, which is far more likely in the summer, this is a great spot for a swim. There are no facilities anywhere on Kauapea and few people – some wearing little or no clothing. This is a traditional "clothing optional" beach.

Snorkeling is best at the northern end of the beach, which requires a long, very sunny hike across one mile of sand to get to the north. While often far too rough, snorkeling can be good on a very calm day. An experienced snorkeler can head out along the point and toward the Moku'ae'ae Island (a bird sanctuary) located off Kilauea Point. This is never the place for beginners since waves can kick up quite suddenly. It's open ocean here with strong currents and no outer reef for protection. If in doubt, play it safe and just enjoy the beach.

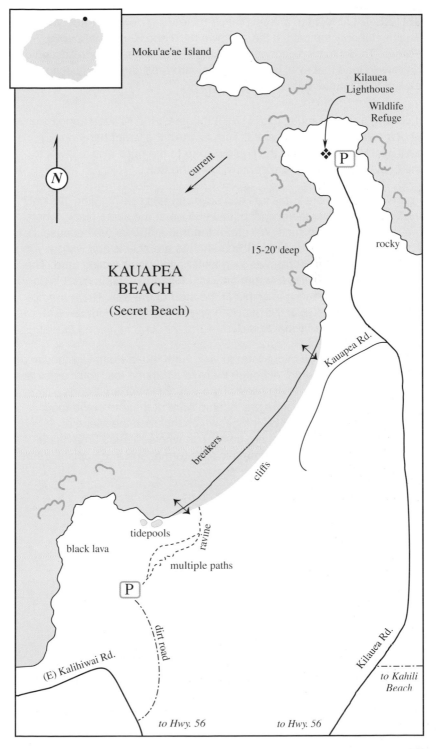

Moku'ae'ae Island

Kilauea
Lighthouse

Wildlife
Refuge

N

current

P

rocky

15-20' deep

KAUAPEA
BEACH

(Secret Beach)

Kauapea Rd.

cliffs

breakers

tidepools

ravine

black lava

multiple paths

P

dirt road

(E) Kalihiwai Rd.

Kilauea Rd.

*to Kahili
Beach*

to Hwy. 56

to Hwy. 56

GETTING THERE There are several paths leading down to Kauapea Beach, but only the path at the southwestern end is legal for public access. To get to the south end of Kauapea, take the eastern section of Kalihiwai Road that exits Highway 56 toward the lighthouse (just southeast of mile marker 24). See map, page 85.

If coming from the south, this is half a mile past the Kilauea turnoff sign, .9 of a mile past mile marker 23. Turn toward the water here on (E) Kalihiwai Road, then take the first dirt road to the right, and follow it to the end, where you can park and will see the trail.

From the parking area, this trail has several branches heading straight, then right down into the ravine, but all end up at the same place, where the ravine meets the sand. We prefer the trail at the far left because it's a bit shorter and easier, but all the branches are scenic and will get you to Kauapea with no problem as long as it hasn't been raining hard. The furthest left trail is still in use, but may be closed eventually, as it is on private property. Parking is ample at the start of the trail. There are no facilities here or down at the beach. If you're going down for several hours, take food and water to last.

While in the area, you might want to visit the Kilauea Point Lighthouse at the end of Kilauea Road. Although there is a parking fee, you'll enjoy the view from this northernmost point of the major Hawai'ian islands. Restrooms and a book store are located here at the end of the road. This is an important Wildlife Refuge, which includes the island of Moku'ae'ae just off the northern point. The whole Kilauea area has a wonderful lush beauty, with dramatic rock formations and tropical greenery in every direction.

Petroglyphs

Sign Language

Any serious snorkeler should bother to learn some basic signs starting with some of the standard Scuba ones: OK – meaning "Are you OK?", which should be answered with another "OK", palm up for "stop", wobbling hand for "problem", thumb down meaning "heading down" (in this case referring to surface diving). This is an essential safety issue making it possible to communicate even if slightly separated. See a few of the signs below.

It's also a nuisance to take the snorkel out of your mouth every time you want to say "Did you see that moray?" Worse yet is trying to understand your buddy who frantically gestures and mumbles through the snorkel while you play charades. With a frequent snorkeling companion it's fun to develop signs for the creatures you might see. Eel can be indicated by three fingers looking like an E or by a wavy line drawn in the water. Then all you have to do it point and there it is!

STOP

PROBLEM

OK

GOING DOWN

COLD

SLOWER

East Area

The east coast of Kaua'i offers pretty bays and beaches one after another along the whole eastern coast. With extensive offshore reefs, there is plenty of snorkeling potential. However, nearly the entire east coast catches the prevailing east swell, making these lovely beaches dangerous most of the year. While we don't recommend snorkeling or swimming when the usual surf is up and the rip currents are ripping, there are some exceptions. The long fringing reef, found offshore along most of the east coast, is a popular fishing and limu (seaweed) collecting spot when the water is calm. This happens only three to four weeks of the year.

When other east coast beaches are foaming with white water, Lydgate State Park near Kapa'a is THE safest snorkeling site in Kaua'i, having a man-made breakwater to stop the waves. Other beaches, like Anahola State Park, offer semi-protected little corners where conditions can be quite calm depending on the exact direction of the swells.

Accommodations can be found at big hotels and condos near Highway 56 in Kapa'a or at house rentals scattered through the towns of the east. Some are very secluded along quiet and uncrowded bays makai (toward the ocean) or mauka (toward the Anahola mountains).

Along Highway 56, you'll find most of the shopping in Kaua'i, with two of its major markets. Golf courses, restaurants, and kayaking are readily available here and several of the rivers offer good kayaking. The rivers are lovely, but can bring lots of silty water to the eastern bays, making them murky when run-off is heavy. The reef offshore is also healthiest where there is less fresh water input.

We've listed some of the major bays and beaches, once again in clockwise order. There are plenty of beautiful spots, especially if you want to get away from the crowds. Most of the best sites will require at least a short hike, if not a long and difficult one. If you are an experienced snorkeler and arrive on an unusually calm day, look over the conditions very carefully before deciding to enter the water.

You'll probably tire of hearing us write about the dangers, but tourists regularly die at these beaches – especially over-confident men (according to the statistics, page 33). We want you to have a delightful and safe snorkeling vacation in Kaua'i. The following east area sites are listed in clockwise order.

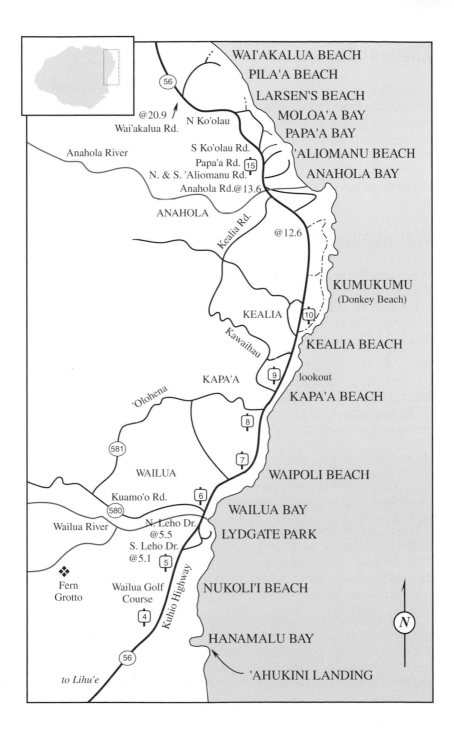

WAI'AKALUA BEACH
PILA'A BEACH
LARSEN'S BEACH
MOLOA'A BAY
PAPA'A BAY
'ALIOMANU BEACH
ANAHOLA BAY

@20.9
Wai'akalua Rd.

N Ko'olau
S Ko'olau Rd.
Papa'a Rd.
N. & S. 'Aliomanu Rd.
Anahola Rd.@13.6

Anahola River

56
15

ANAHOLA

Kealia Rd.

@12.6

KUMUKUMU
(Donkey Beach)

KEALIA

Kawaihau

10

KEALIA BEACH

KAPA'A

9

lookout

KAPA'A BEACH

'Olohena

8

581

7

WAIPOLI BEACH

WAILUA

6

Kuamo'o Rd.

580

WAILUA BAY

Wailua River

N. Leho Dr.
@5.5
S. Leho Dr.
@5.1

LYDGATE PARK

5

Fern
Grotto

Wailua Golf
Course

Kuhio Highway

NUKOLI'I BEACH

4

HANAMALU BAY

N

56

to Lihu'e

'AHUKINI LANDING

89

Kilauea Bay (Kahili Beach, Quarry Beach)

Strong currents and undertow make this beach too dangerous for most snorkelers. The river can add to the danger. Kilauea Bay faces northeast picking up swells from both directions. Both the road and paths get slippery after heavy rains. It's better to leave this one to locals who are more familiar with the changing conditions. We've been told that there is good snorkeling when conditions are calm, but we have not snorkeled this site.

Wai'akalua Beach

While this is a pretty beach (actually two beaches) and the hike isn't long, it usually isn't a good snorkeling destination. The reef catches eastern swells making it impossible to snorkel outside the reef most of the year. You'll be able to check out conditions from the bluff where the hike begins.

Inside the reef, where it's calm, you'll find the water often too shallow for pleasant swimming or snorkeling. It might be worth a try at high tide, but we didn't think it looked promising except perhaps to snorkel near the boulders at either end of the beach. Stay away from any stream channels when swells are pounding the reef because all that water has to get out somewhere. You sure don't want to get swept out along with it.

Snorkeling is best around the point to the right toward Pila'a, but you'll have to get awfully lucky to find it calm enough.

If you're just looking for a spot for a picnic, then Wai'akalua might fill the bill. It must have been a lovely secluded spot before houses and roads came down here, but it now feels developed. The trail down is especially steep, and slippery when wet. Of course, there are no facilities here.

GETTING THERE From Highway 56, you'll need to turn toward the ocean on North Wai'akalua Road (at mile 20.9). Head toward the ocean for .7 of a mile (see map, page 93), then turn left on a dirt road just before the end of the road. Continue on the dirt road lined with ironwoods to the end for .2 of a mile. You can park here and catch a good view of the little bays below.

Doctor My Eyes

If you are swimming along snorkeling peacefully and your vision suddenly loses focus, don't be too quick to panic and call for a doctor. While you may have had a stroke or the water may be oily, there is a much more likely cause: You've probably just entered into an outdoor demonstration of the refractive qualities of mixtures of clear liquids of different densities. Is that perfectly clear?

Near the edge of some protected bays, clear spring water oozes smoothly out into the saltwater. As it is lighter than the mineral-laden saltwater, it tends to float in a layer near the surface for a time.

Now, clear spring water is easy to see through, as is clear saltwater. If you mix them thoroughly, you have dilute saltwater, still clear. But when the two float side by side, the light going through them is bent and re-bent as it passes between them, and this blurs your vision. It's much like the blurring produced when hot, lighter air rises off black pavement, and produces wavy vision and mirage.

These lenses of clear water drift about, and often disappear as quickly as they appeared. Swimming away from the source of the spring water usually solves the problem. Clear at last?

The path is steep, slippery and about 200 yards long. When wet, it would be nearly impossible. At the bottom of the bluff, you need to hike another 400 yards to the beach to your left. Hike along the sand (which pretty much disappears when swell is high.)

Pila'a Beach

The next beach located south of Wai'akalua is Pila'a. This one also catches the eastern swell and will be dangerous most days of the year. It also requires a long and difficult hike over some boulders from below, or bushwhacking from on top. The inner protected area is very shallow, so high tide is the best bet even on a good day. All in all, too dangerous and difficult to be worth the long hike.

Larsen's Beach

While east-facing beaches in Kaua'i tend to catch waves most of the year, you might get lucky and come here and find flat water. If so, this is one of the best and longest beaches on this side of the island.

Walking down involves only an easy five-minute stroll from the low hills down the gradual slope. The trail can get slippery after a heavy rain, but isn't dangerous or difficult.

The broad main trail leads to the center of the beach while other branches lead both north and south. This is a dry, somewhat windswept, area with plenty of sand. Pretty clusters of beach heliotrope and kiawe trees line the beach.

The outer reef protecting the beach gets waves most of the year, but the inner area provides safe, but shallow, snorkeling. High tide is definitely best if you like some clearance. Avoid the channels if there's any hint of currents sweeping out to sea. From the parking area, you may be able to see the rapids in the largest center channel. Stay well away from anything that looks like that! It's unlikely there will be anyone here to rescue you if you get caught in one of the rip currents. If in doubt, stay out of the water. These beaches exposed to the east swell are all for advanced snorkelers only – at any time of the year because conditions can change suddenly. Take a long look and imagine what would happen to a snorkeler if a set of large waves suddenly crossed the reef. Winter and spring tend to be particularly dangerous on this side of Kaua'i, but the east can have huge waves and wicked currents at any time of the year.

Still, Larsen's Beach is worth the short, pretty hike and offers parking under the ironwoods, picnicking under the kukui trees, and a nice stroll along the beach. You'll see some beach heliotrope thriving in this dry and windy location. This long, shallow reef is a popular limu (seaweed) harvesting site.

GETTING THERE Ko'olau Road has a north and south exit from Highway 56. The north end is at mile marker 20 (see map, page 93) and is the closest. Heading toward the ocean from the northern end of Ko'olau Road, go 1.2 miles, then take a dirt road to your left. There's an easily missed pipe with "beach access" on it. Continue on this dirt road for .9 of a mile to the end, where you can park and look down on Larsen's beach. Multiple paths lead down to this long beach. Take your pick: center, left or right. The hike is easy, broad and sunny – about 300 yards to the water. To get here from the south end of Ko'olau Road, go toward the ocean from Highway 56 at marker 16, then pass the road to Moloa'a

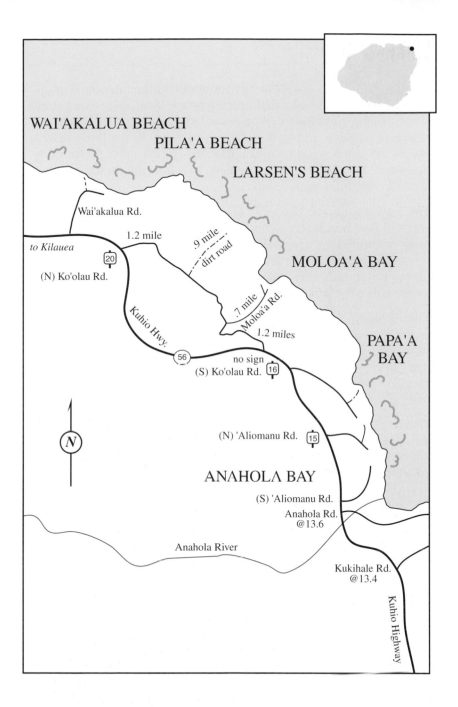

WAI'AKALUA BEACH

PILA'A BEACH

LARSEN'S BEACH

Wai'akalua Rd.

1.2 mile

.9 mile
dirt road

to Kilauea

[20]

(N) Ko'olau Rd.

MOLOA'A BAY

Kuhio Hwy.

.7 mile

Moloa'a Rd.

1.2 miles

[56]

no sign

(S) Ko'olau Rd. [16]

PAPA'A
BAY

(N) 'Aliomanu Rd. [15]

ANAHOLA BAY

(S) 'Aliomanu Rd.

Anahola Rd.
@13.6

Anahola River

Kukihale Rd.
@13.4

Kuhio Highway

Bay, till you come to the dirt road on your right with a pipe that says
"beach access." Head .9 of a mile to the end of the dirt road, where you
can park and get a good view of the beach.

Moloa'a Bay

A beautiful bay set down low in lush surroundings. Access is complicated by all the houses that line the beach. Still, once you get out to the beach, your effort will be rewarded. Park along the street wherever possible, and walk as far as you must. While these eastern beaches in general can be rough, this one is a bit more protected by outer reef. It's also one of the prettiest, in a lush jungle setting protected by the hills on three sides.

The road stops at the houses in about the middle of the bay where you will find beach access, but the water here is too rocky for swimming or snorkeling. Try walking along the sand to the picturesque far northern end (to your left) or the far southern end for somewhat calmer water with safer entry. Watch the direction of the swells before choosing which way to hike.

There's plenty of sand and space for secluded picnicking at either end of the beach. The bay's horseshoe shape helps stop the swells from most directions, but you still need to be cautious about currents sweeping out from the center. When calm enough, there is excellent snorkeling throughout the bay. But never, ever venture beyond the points.

Watch mainly for rip currents when waves are pounding the coral at the mouth of the bay. All that water has to somehow sweep back to sea and it usually does so from the center of the bay. No facilities are available here.

GETTING THERE From the south, take Highway 56 past Anahola, take the southern end of Ko'olau Road to the right (toward the ocean) at mile marker 16 (see map, page 93). Go 1.2 miles on this unmarked road, then turn right on Moloa'a Road. Follow Moloa'a for .7 of a mile and park where you find space near the end of the road. There aren't many parking spaces near the houses, so be sure you don't block access to homes. You may need to double back to find parking along the road.

Continue walking from the end of the road to the far north. Depending on conditions, you may want to park further south and walk to the south end of the bay. The area right in the middle is too shallow for good snorkeling and often rougher.

From the north, take Highway 56 to mile marker 20 to find the northern end of Ko'olau Road. Turn toward the water here on Ko'olau and go 2.3 miles, then turn left on Moloa'a Road for another .7 of a mile.

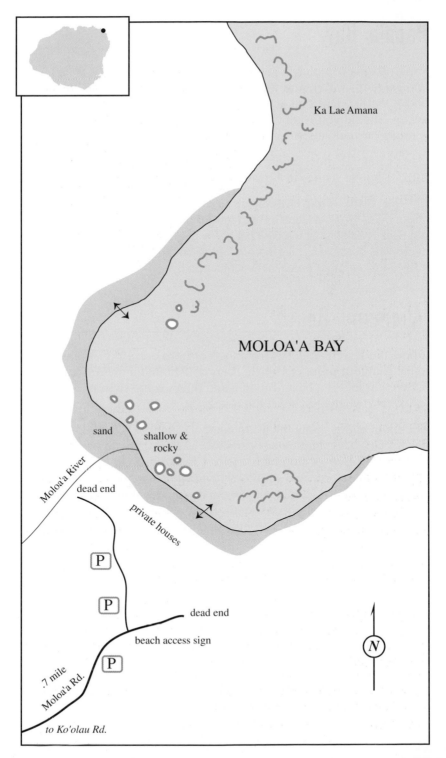

Ka Lae Amana

MOLOA'A BAY

sand

shallow &
rocky

Moloa'a River

dead end

private houses

P

P

dead end

beach access sign

P

.7 mile
Moloa'a Rd.

to Ko'olau Rd.

N

Papa'a Bay

Papa'a Bay is completely surrounded by private property. It's a lush and gorgeous valley, and was used as the set for the movie "6 Days and 7 Nights." Difficult access makes it hard to recommend for snorkeling. Should you want to hike in, the beach is picturesque, but has a strong current sweeping out from the center.

One of Kaua'i's most scenic spots, Papa'a Bay also provided the setting for jungle scenes in Jurassic Park.

GETTING THERE From Highway 56, just north of 'Aliomanu and south of mile marker 16, take Papa'a Road toward the ocean (see map, page 93). This road ends at the bay, but has a guard posted to keep out the public. It is possible to hike in from further south, but it's a long difficult hike. Consider other beautiful beaches nearby.

'Aliomanu Beach

'Aliomanu Beach stretches from the northern corner of Anahola Bay to the southern point of Papa'a. Parts of 'Aliomanu are difficult to access, but this is a beautiful area and offers some swimming and snorkeling when seas aren't too rough.

The south end is along the north edge of Anahola Bay and attracts few beach-goers. The water near shore is studded with rocks and not very deep, so swimming is tricky. Check our map (page 97) for a lovely spot to picnic and snorkel when calm. Always err on the side of caution. Since Anahola is a large bay, you'll want to drive here rather than hike from the far south. Be sure to stay well away from the river which may cause strong currents at any time of the year.

There is a long and wide fringing reef here, where collecting limu (seaweed) is very popular. 'Aliomanu provides the sought-after pink variety, so you may see people harvesting it out on the reef. This particular seaweed grows where the surf pounds, so don't try picking any yourself!

GETTING THERE From Highway 56, take the north section of 'Aliomanu Road toward the ocean when you see the highway marker 15 (see map, page 97). Turn left on Kikana as you approach the bay. Otherwise you will come to the dead end. Kikana itself will also dead end at a pretty and relatively calm section of 'Aliomanu Beach.

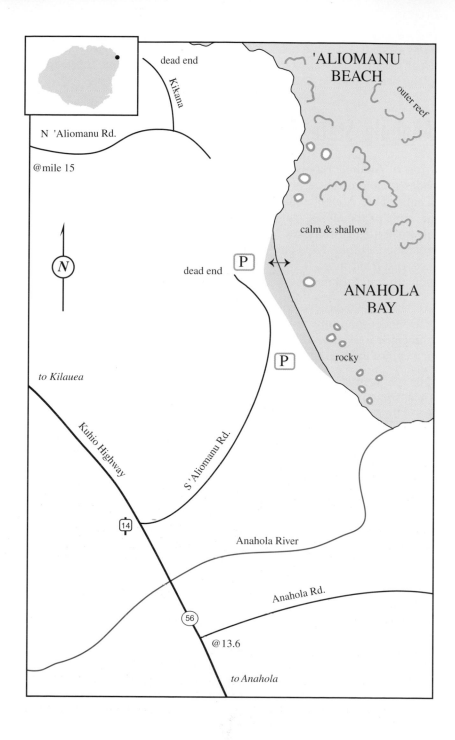

dead end

Kikana

N 'Aliomanu Rd.

@mile 15

'ALIOMANU
BEACH

outer reef

N

calm & shallow

P ↔

dead end

ANAHOLA
BAY

P

rocky

to Kilauea

Kuhio Highway

S 'Aliomanu Rd.

14

Anahola River

Anahola Rd.

56

@13.6

to Anahola

For the south end of the beach, take the south segment of 'Aliomanu Road toward the ocean. It too will dead end. 'Aliomanu Road is another of the beach roads in Kaua'i that have been cut in two by tsunamis.

Anahola State Park

Most of Anahola Bay is exposed to the eastern swells. Its angle provides some protection, with the southern corner usually calmest. That's where Anahola State Park is located, with restrooms, showers, parking, picnic tables, camping and a lifeguard station (but not always a lifeguard). Local families like to camp in the lovely setting near the facilities. Kids play in the shallow calm water and their parents fish from shore. This is a Hawai'ian Homelands area, so be particularly careful to not be an obnoxious tourist, and you'll do alright.

At the far southeastern corner, where the water is calmest, you can park under the ironwoods, relax on the heliotrope-lined sandy beach and enjoy a terrific view of the Anahola Mountains. This southeastern end of the bay has only a narrow ribbon of sand.

The reef near shore is very shallow, so high tide is a must. Even then, some people will find it too shallow for comfort. This is a good time to wear a wetsuit if you have one.

There is a small channel you can locate on our map to snorkel without skimming the reef quite so closely. While snorkeling within the reef isn't spectacular, there are plenty of fish and the setting is excellent. Entry from the sand is easy and there is usually little or no current at this end. When big waves roll into the bay, it's wise to check for any outgoing currents in the small channel.

When calm, you can snorkel beyond the inner reef – even around the point at the far right. It's wise to check with the lifeguard before venturing out this far. While local visitors might suggest it's no problem, keep in mind that they know the ocean here better than you do. Venture beyond the inner reef only when you're sure it's entirely safe. Most of the bay is only about twenty feet deep.

Skimming the reef we saw needlefish, pink coral, interesting sea slugs, and a variety of tangs. We particularly enjoyed close-up views of butterflyfish including the lined, oval, four-spot and raccoon.

A shower is available at this end of the beach, although it's a simple pole that's easy to miss, so check the location on our map. Back near the lifeguard station you'll find restrooms and another shower. Bring a picnic lunch and relax in one of Kaua'i's magical settings with

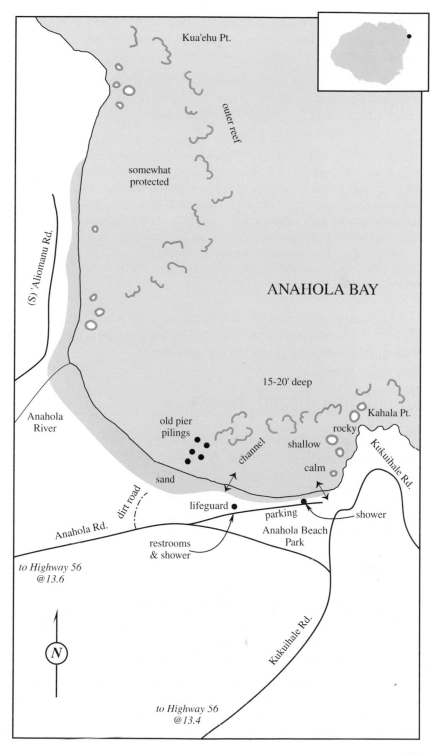

Kua'ehu Pt.

outer reef

somewhat
protected

(S) 'Aliomanu Rd.

ANAHOLA BAY

15-20' deep

Anahola
River

old pier
pilings

Kahala Pt.

rocky

channel

shallow

Kukuihale Rd.

sand

calm

dirt road

lifeguard

parking

shower

Anahola Rd.

restrooms
& shower

Anahola Beach
Park

to Highway 56
@13.6

N

Kukuihale Rd.

to Highway 56
@13.4

99

birds singing in the treetops. We always enjoy relaxing here. Come here for the natural beauty, and enjoy a little snorkeling if the tide is high enough.

At the opposite end of Anahola Bay you'll find more lovely beach with wider sand, but rougher water. There are no facilities at this end, but snorkeling is possible toward the point at the left. This is another good spot for a picnic.

GETTING THERE From the south, head north on Highway 56, turning right (toward the water) on Kukuihale Road at mile 13.4 (see map, page 99). Continue to the left when you come to a Y, then double back almost immediately at the next Y where you'll need to turn right. This road will lead you into the park where you'll find plenty of parking with facilities near the center. A sign will say "Welcome to Anahola Beach Park." The best snorkeling is at the far southeastern end of the beach. To park close, just drive to the very end of the road and park under the iron-woods.

Coming from the north, turn left on Anahola Road (at mile 13.6). Follow this road .7 of a mile to the beach, staying right at the first Y, then left at the second Y, where you'll see the welcome sign.

Kumukumu Beach (Donkey Beach)

We've seen Kumukumu Beach recommended as a snorkeling and swimming destination. We do not see it that way. You'll have a long hike to get to the beach, access may be blocked, then you will almost certainly encounter strong currents, big waves, and danger-ous undertow. It is well-known as an unofficial swimsuits-optional beach and is more suited to sunbathing than water sports. Needless to say, this is for experts only.

The name Donkey Beach comes from the days when donkeys roamed the pastures above the beach.

GETTING THERE Taking Highway north from Kealia, take a right at mile 12.6 (see map, page 101). This road will wind back along the eastern beaches. While it's seldom safe for swimming, you'll find a beach at Kumukumu and snorkeling spots around the rocks to the north. Kumukumu is located approximately 1.5 miles north of Kealia and 2 miles south of Anahola Bay.

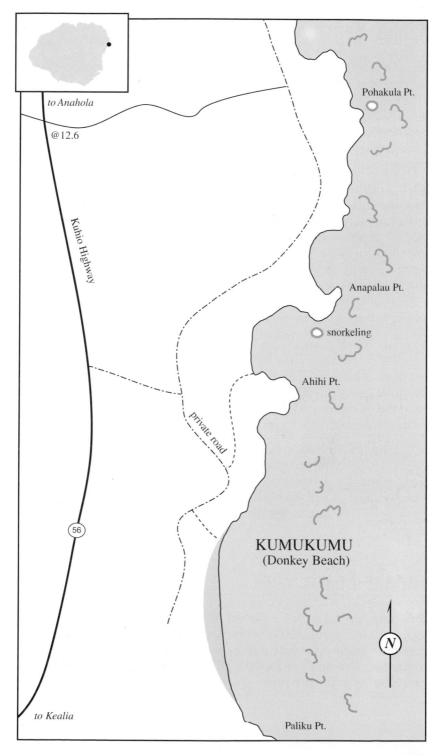

to Anahola

@12.6

Kuhio Highway

Pohakula Pt.

Anapalau Pt.

○ snorkeling

Ahihi Pt.

private road

56

KUMUKUMU
(Donkey Beach)

N

to Kealia

Paliku Pt.

Kealia Beach

Most of this long stretch of beach is very rough and dangerous, but the northern end is somewhat protected by a short breakwater and offers a lovely beach. When calm enough, snorkel toward the end of the breakwater and then turn south for about 100 yards. You'll pass by a very large anchor (about ten feet across). Even if the entry is safe, waves will decrease visibility. Sometimes stingrays can be seen cruising along the sandy bottom.

Snorkeling the south end is possible ONLY if the waves are very low (less than one foot). A popular dive site is found about 200 feet from the south point, where there's a ledge under about 15 feet of water and another under about 25 feet. The water out here is often clear and it's just shallow enough for snorkeling. Look for the boulders encrusted with coral. Divers call this Kealia Kitchen. You will probably see turtles, parrotfish, longnose butterflyfish and the pretty Picasso triggerfish. It's great snorkeling, but the catch is that it's calm only a few weeks of the year.

You'll definitely want to avoid the river toward the center of the beach. This beach is close to the highway, so you can look out to check on conditions. The beach is somewhat bare with little shade, but quite beautiful. Kealia Beach is a nice place to walk, bike along the path, or explore tidepools. Parking is found in several spots makai of the highway, but no other facilities are available.

GETTING THERE   Between Kapa'a and Kumukumu, you'll find Kealia Beach. To get there, go north on Highway 56 past Kapa'a. After crossing the Mo'ikeha Canal (see map, page 103), watch for turnouts along the makai (ocean) side of the highway near mile marker 10. You'll have a good view of the area before deciding whether it's safe to swim or snorkel.

Kapa'a Beach Park

This long beach along the edge of Kapa'a has easy access with restrooms and picnic tables in the center. You'll need to check out ocean conditions carefully and look for the spot that offers the best protection. Both ends of the beach are somewhat protected as is the center near the jetty. Which is best will depend on the exact angle of the swells.

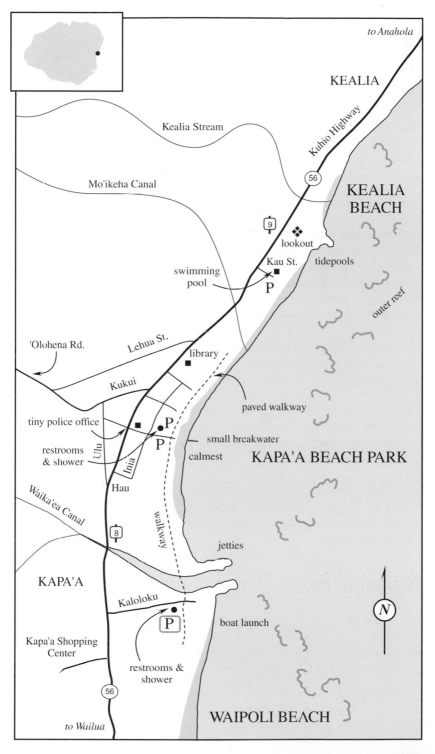

to Anahola

KEALIA

Kealia Stream

Mo'ikeha Canal

Kuhio Highway

56

KEALIA
BEACH

9

lookout

Kau St.

tidepools

swimming
pool

P

outer reef

'Olohena Rd.

Lehua St.

library

Kukui

paved walkway

tiny police office

P

restrooms
& shower

P

small breakwater

Ulu

Inia

calmest

KAPA'A BEACH PARK

Hau

Waika'ea Canal

walkway

8

jetties

KAPA'A

Kaloloku

P

boat launch

Kapa'a Shopping
Center

N

restrooms &
shower

56

WAIPOLI BEACH

to Wailua

103

Kapa'a is a long beach requiring a drive to either end and has parking in several locations. You'll find a paved walkway along most of the south and center beach. Clumps of ironwoods and coconut palms provide some needed shade. You'll find scattered picnic areas as well as a boat ramp into the canal near the southern end of the beach.

Snorkeling is better at the northern end of the beach when conditions are good, but there are no facilities at this end. As usual in Kaua'i, stay well away from channels and rivers, where the snorkeling will be too murky anyway.

GETTING THERE Kapa'a Beach Park is found along the east of the city of Kapa'a. The center has the best parking, as well as restrooms and shower. To get here, turn toward the water at the tiny police station on the corner of Highway 56 (see map, page 103). You'll find restrooms and parking here as well as a walkway running in both directions along the beach. The small breakwater right in front offers some protection to its right. The outer reef here generally provides some protection from the worst of the eastern swells.

Kapa'a is a long beach with a paved walkway most of the way, so walk to the calmest area before considering entering the water. Parking is also available at several other spots along the beach.

To get to the boat ramp in the south, take Kaloloku from Highway 56 toward the water. You'll find plenty of parking, restrooms, and shower near the boat ramp. Since this park is so long, you may want to scout it out by car first.

Yet another entrance from Highway 56 is located at mile marker 9 further north. This one takes you to the Kapa'a public swimming pool and tennis courts near another somewhat calmer area. No facilities here except for parking.

Waipouli Beach Park

Just south of Kapa'a, you'll find small Waipouli Beach County Park, where seas are rough most of the year. It's a nice place to walk along the path that connects it to Kapa'a. Depending on the season, you may find little pockets of sand that are calmer.

GETTING THERE Waipouli is just south of Kapa'a – across the Waika'ea Canal (see map, page 103). You can walk the beach from Kapa'a or drive around to get to Waipouli Beach Park.

Wailua Beach

At the mouth of the Wailua River you'll find the beach with showers and restrooms. This is a popular kayaking spot, but has heavy run-off from the river and catches some large eastern swells. It's definitely not a good swimming or snorkeling site most of the year.

GETTING THERE Located toward the ocean from the town of Wailua, this park is easy to find – located at mile marker 6 on Highway 56 near the Coconut Palms Resort.

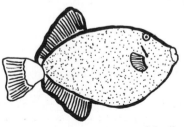

pinktail triggerfish

Lydgate Beach Park

Lydgate is Kaua'i's calmest and safest year-round snorkeling beach. A man-made lava wall protects this beach from all trade wind-driven swell. A delightful and easy snorkeling site – perfect for beginners and children. For you more advanced snorkelers, it's also a chance to get very close to some beautiful fish that have learned to hang out with people. There's something here for everyone and it's an attractive full-service park as well. Plenty of parking, lifeguards, several restrooms and showers, expanses of grass and sand, covered picnic areas, and even a fish ID display. All this adds to the main attraction – the fish.

The central snorkeling pond ranges from 3-6' deep and is large enough that it doesn't feel crowded. Another pond just to the north offers an even shallower spot for toddlers to play safely. When and if they're done playing in the water, there's a children's park mauka.

For snorkeling at Lydgate, low tide brings clearer water. Most of the bottom is sand, so you don't have to sorry about skimming the coral. Just wander around the scattered coral heads.

It's annoying to see people here still feeding the fish, but signs are beginning to discourage this practice. You may notice that black surgeonfish and large chubs are more numerous at sites where people regularly feed the fish. These aggressive fish can easily crowd out some of the more colorful ones.

Middle of the day brings the crowds to Lydgate, so you may prefer mornings or late afternoon.. There could hardly be a better place to learn how to snorkel with absolutely no worries about swells or difficult entry. And the fish are large and exciting. We saw an excellent variety of butterflyfish, tangs, wrasses and even some large parrotfish. Big chubs also swim about looking for handouts. My favorites here are the scrawled filefish showing off their blue scribbled sides and the neon multi-colored yellowtail coris.

GETTING THERE From Lihu'e, heading north on Highway 56, turn right on Leho Drive toward the ocean (see map, page 89) just north of the Wailua Golf Course. This is .5 of a mile north of mile marker 5. Go .3 of a mile on Leho, then turn left on Nalu Road. From here it's just .2 of a mile to the park. You'll see the park entrance to the north and can easily find plenty of parking close to the water. You'll find all facilities in the center.

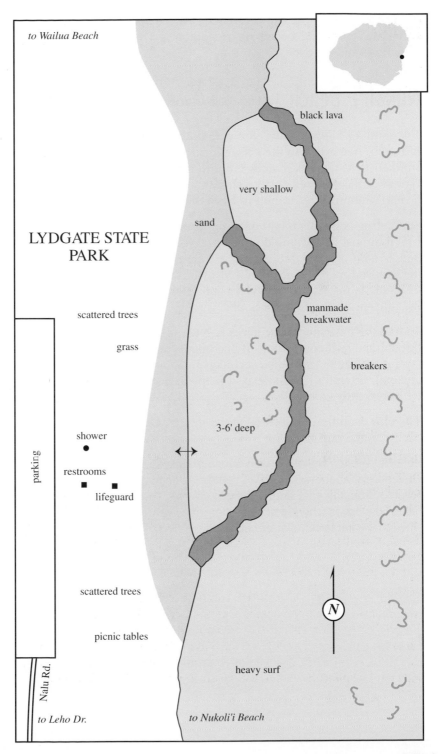

to Wailua Beach

black lava

very shallow

sand

LYDGATE STATE
PARK

manmade
breakwater

breakers

scattered trees

grass

3-6' deep

shower

restrooms

lifeguard

parking

scattered trees

picnic tables

N

Nalu Rd.

to Leho Dr.

to Nukoli'i Beach

heavy surf

It's a bit longer, but you can also reach Lydgate from the southern end of Leho Drive by turning toward the ocean at mile 5.1. Then turn right on Nalu Road into the park.

Nukoli'i Beach (Wailua Golf Course)

Just south of Lydgate Park, you will find this two-mile long stretch of beach. According to the lifeguards at Lydgate, it's calm enough for snorkeling for approximately seven to ten days of the year (probably typical of the exposed eastern shore). Waves can really pound the beach, when rolling straight in from the east.

Snorkeling is good straight out from the golf course, but you have to find it almost flat. If you do, go for it! Advanced snorkelers could handle a bit of swell, but should still be extra careful anywhere on the exposed east side of Kaua'i. Most of the exposed eastern shore of Kaua'i is for expert snorkelers only. Beginners should stay within the fully-protected Lydgate pools.

To find the best snorkeling spots at Nukoli'i, take the paved road through the golf course until it becomes a dirt road. Follow this road toward the sea to find some secluded little coves for the safest entry and exit. To find the same exit, it helps to mark your entrance point with a brightly colored bag.

The only facilities are located at the nearby Outrigger Hilton. In the ocean, found golf balls are free.

GETTING THERE   Nukoli'i Beach is located just south of Lydgate Park. It stretches for about two miles with entrance either from the Outrigger Hilton or from the east side of the golf course. The rocky coast here offers little coves where you can enter the water from a bit of sand only when the water is completely calm.

yellow tang

Leptospirosis

Signs along the Kalihiwai River warn of the danger of lepto-spirosis, a bacterial disease that can be transmitted from animals to humans in fresh water. You may wonder what they're talking about!

Although this isn't a common disease (there are about 12 cases reported on Kaua'i each year), it pays to at least know the symptoms if you're going to find yourself in any fresh water activity here on Kaua'i. It's a risk worth bearing in mind if you plan to spend much time playing in rivers. Snorkeling is better in the sea anyway!

The disease is spread through animal urine, particularly from mice and rats. It can be found in any fresh water on Kaua'i, so it's best to avoid the rivers if you have open cuts. Keep your head out of the fresh water if boating. And, certainly, do not drink any stream water on the island.

Symptoms can begin anywhere from two to twenty days after exposure. They include high fever, diarrhea, vomiting, chills, headache, body pain and weakness. Since mild cases resemble the flu, they're unlikely to be diagnosed correctly. If left untreated, more serious cases can cause kidney failure, jaundice or heart failure.

If you develop a high fever a week after fresh water activities, lepto should be looked at as a possible cause.

Should you develop any of these symptoms, tell your doctor about possible leptospirosis exposure. Early treatment with antibiotics is important. For some odd reason, kids under 10 very rarely get lepto. Teens who play on rope swings into rivers are at higher risk, as is anyone who enjoys an activity likely to give them skin abrasions.

Your best protection is to wear clothing that protects your skin when in fresh water – running around barefoot is risky, for example, as you could easily cut your foot while in the water.

We don't think the risk from leptospirosis is high enough to warrant avoiding fresh water swimming entirely. But it might be better to spend your time swimming in the ocean than playing for hours in the fresh water rivers and lagoons. For more information, call the Kaua'i District Health Office: 808-241-3563.

Lihu'e Area

The Lihu'e area near the airport is mostly hidden from the highway, but offers Kaua'i's deepest and most sheltered bays – Hanama'ulu and Nawiliwili. These bays provide considerably calmer water than the beaches exposed to the full eastern swell. While surf can pick up here as well, there's often a chance of finding excellent conditions. These beaches can be shielded from prevailing east swells, winter north swells and summer south swells.

The Marriott is located on wide sandy Kalapaki Beach and has some public access. Parking is the biggest challenge here, so come early unless you're staying at the Marriott.

The Lihu'e area offers a convenient central location near the airport, where you can head either north or south, depending on the day's weather.

Hanama'ulu Beach Park

The visibility here is very poor. While it improves as you swim out, it's still not the best snorkeling site. A very strong swimmer, however, may want to snorkel all the way to 'Ahukini Landing.

The beach park is a pretty site with a river and shallow area where children play in calm weather. There's shade under the ironwoods. Amenities include showers, restrooms, picnic tables and camping.

GETTING THERE From the town of Hanama'ulu, take Hehi Road to the beach, located where the Hanama'ulu River enters the bay. This is just north of the Lihu'e Airport (see map, page 111).

reef squid

110

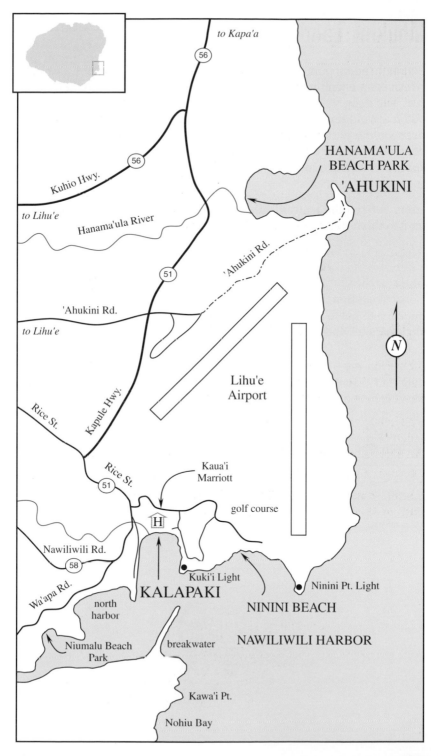

to Kapa'a

56

HANAMA'ULA
BEACH PARK
'AHUKINI

56

Kuhio Hwy.

to Lihu'e

Hanama'ula River

'Ahukini Rd.

51

'Ahukini Rd.

to Lihu'e

N

Lihu'e
Airport

Rice St.

Kapule Hwy.

Rice St.

Kaua'i
Marriott

51

golf course

H

Nawiliwili Rd.

Kuki'i Light

58

KALAPAKI

Ninini Pt. Light

Wa'apa Rd.

north
harbor

NININI BEACH

Niumalu Beach
Park

breakwater

NAWILIWILI HARBOR

Kawa'i Pt.

Nohiu Bay

'Ahukini Landing

Out past the airport, you can drive all the way to 'Ahukini Landing, which is an excellent spot for fishing and has been a popular dive site. The deep water provides excellent visibility. Signs are now posted on the old jetty that say "no snorkeling or scuba diving." The area between the jetty and the breakwater is well-protected.Certainly this deep water site is not for beginners and also not for those who fear sharks. You'll also have to be extremely careful about currents heading toward the ocean.

Entry is from the leeward side of the old jetty, where the water is fifteen to thirty feet deep. This is boulder habitat rather than coral and a chance to see pelagic fish – even sharks if you're lucky. Snorkel at your own risk.

GETTING THERE   'Ahukini Landing is across the Hanama'ula Bay from Hanama'ula Beach Park, but you need to drive through the airport entrance to get to it unless you don't mind the long swim from Hanama'ula Beach Park.

From Highway 51, take the airport exit called 'Ahukini Road (see map, page 111). Continue on this road, staying left, past the airport, past UPS, past the heliport, as it meanders to the end where you'll find the breakwater. It's 1.8 miles from the highway and slow going, but a pretty spot that's worth the drive. 'Ahukini Landing is at the end of the road by the old pier, where a prominent sign says "no snorkeling or scuba diving."

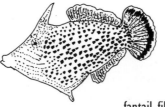

fantail filefish

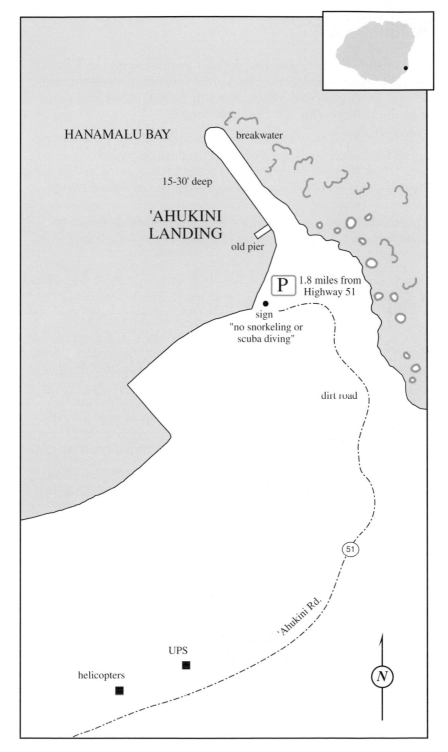

HANAMALU BAY

breakwater

15-30' deep

'AHUKINI
LANDING

old pier

P 1.8 miles from
Highway 51

sign
"no snorkeling or
scuba diving"

dirt road

51

'Ahukini Rd.

UPS

helicopters

N

Ninini Beach

This small beach is tucked into the cliff area to the east of Kalapaki Beach. It's seldom calm, but offers good snorkeling along the cliff when the rare calm day arrives. You will need to either hike down from the cliff or swim from Kalapaki Beach.

GETTING THERE Follow the directions to Kalapaki Beach (and see map, page 111), but continue on Ho'olaulea Way past the hotel to the upper area, where there are several marked public parking areas located along the road. A variety of paths lead down the cliff, but all require caution.

It's probably easier to swim from the east end of Kalapaki Beach and avoid the hike over rocks, but it's a long swim and only for experienced snorkelers.

Kalapaki Beach (Nawiliwili Beach Park)

This large protected cove within Nawiliwili Bay sits in front of the Kaua'i Marriott. It's a lovely setting with river at the western corner and sheer cliffs bordering the eastern end of the bay. Parking and all facilities are available at the public park near the river, but snorkelers would be better off at the eastern end, where limited public access is provided by the hotel. Since parking spots here fill early, come by 9 a.m. to use this end of the beach. Otherwise you'll have to wade through the river and hike the full length of Kalapaki Beach.

In spite of the protection within Nawiliwili Bay, swells can and do pick up – especially in the winter. Usually though, you'll find Kalapaki much calmer than most of the eastern coast. Kalapaki Beach is popular for swimming, snorkeling, and kayaking.

On calm days, park in the hotel spots designated for the public (see map, page 115) and snorkel the eastern end of the beach out along the cliffs toward Kuki'i Point. If it's very calm, try going around the point, but always stop if you encounter any current or big swells.

Kapapaki is a delightful spot where you can lounge on grass or sand under the palm trees with restrooms inside the unlikely-looking building to your left. Showers are near the sand.

For a quick trip up to the bluff, take the elevator within the building where the restrooms are located. It will take you to the upper area lagoon, but it's still a long, hot hike to the edge of the bluff, then a scramble over rocks if you want to snorkel Ninini Beach.

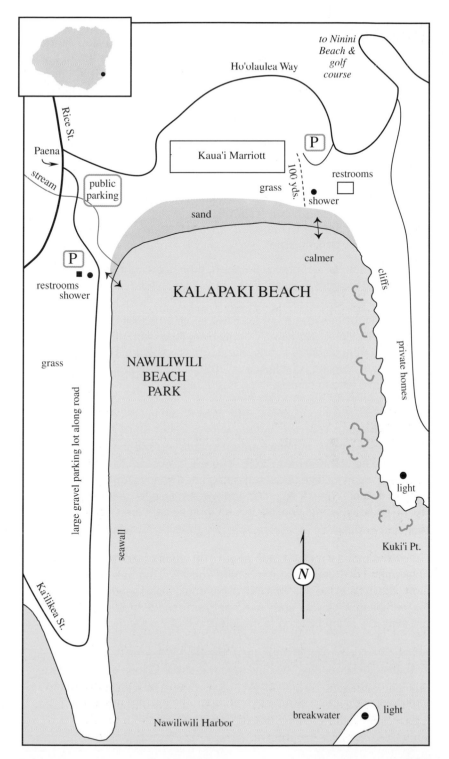

to Ninini
Beach &
golf
course

Ho'olaulea Way

Rice St.

Kaua'i Marriott

P

Paena

stream

public
parking

restrooms

grass

100 yds.

shower

sand

calmer

P

restrooms
shower

KALAPAKI BEACH

cliffs

private homes

grass

NAWILIWILI
BEACH
PARK

large gravel parking lot along road

seawall

light

Kuki'i Pt.

Ka'ilikea St.

Nawiliwili Harbor

breakwater

light

115

Better yet, drive up the road to find several spots up the hill toward the east where you can have a great view of Nawiliwili Bay. Some parking areas have paths down to the water, but none of the paths are easy since most of this corner is very rocky. It's better to enjoy the view or a short hike than try to climb over the rocks to snorkel near the entrance of Nawiliwili Bay, Kaua'i's main port. As we write, this upper area looks somewhat abandoned – especially the shopping center near the point.

GETTING THERE
Kalapaki Beach can be reached from the west or east. The popular public beach with facilities is located at the western end of the bay where the river empties into the bay. From the north, on Highway 50, take Rice Street (Highway 51) toward the water (see map, page 111). Watch carefully and turn toward the water on Paena into the fair-sized public parking area.

From the south, take Highway 56 north, then head right on Rice Street (Highway 51) toward the water. Paena will be on your left.

Or, to avoid the crowds, arrive from the south on Ka'ilikea Street where you will see signs to Nawiliwili County Park (see map, page 115). The park here offers plenty of shade, sand, grass, showers, restrooms, and picnic tables. Parking is usually available along the road by the seawall – since people tend to come and go frequently.

For the best snorkeling access, take Rice Street in Lihu'e (Highway 51) toward the water. Then turn left toward the Kaua'i Marriott on Ho'olaulea Way. Drive east past the hotel entrance until you see the public access sign to the right at Kalapaki Circle. You will drop down to the Marriott's eastern parking lot with about ten designated spaces for the public in the eastern corner. When these fill, people seem able to park along the road. The hotel seems to allow this as long as cars aren't blocking the road.

Follow the broad flagstone path about 100 yards south to the lovely eastern end of Kalapaki Beach, where you'll find the best snorkeling along the cliffs at the left This half of Kalapaki also seems a bit calmer for swimming. Pick your spot: sand or grass, shade or sun. Restrooms are available in the building to the left (east) of the sand.

Although seldom calm enough for snorkeling, the area beyond the eastern cliffs can be reached by driving to the upper lagoon area, where a number of steep paths lead down to the water. You'll find designated parking spaces up here too – even though the lots are nearly empty. This is worth a drive just for the view of Nawiliwili Bay.

To walk from the eastern end of Kalapaki Beach, simply walk into the building with the restrooms and take the elevator to the upper level. You'll have a long hike to the beach, but it's a lovely view from the top.

Niumalu Beach Park

This beach further inside Nawiliwili Bay is fine for camping and kayaking, but there is too much fresh water run-off with its poor visibility, so you won't find good snorkeling here.

GETTING THERE   From Kalapaki Beach, head southwest on Wa'ape Road or Niumalu Road. You'll find the park just to the west of the main harbor (see map, page 111).

Disposable Underwater Cameras

Cheap, widely available, even stocked on some excursions, and fun to use. Keep your expectations realistic and you won't end up disappointed, although you won't get pictures like you see in National Geographic. The professionals who get all those great shots use camera setups worth $10,000 and more. They also have assistants underwater to hold the lights and spare cameras. Their books start to look like bargains compared with trying to get these pictures by yourself. Check out the great selection of marine life books in Kaua'i bookstores.

Still, it's fun to try for that cute shot of your sweetie in a bikini, clowning with the fish. If you're lucky, you'll actually have identifiable fish in a few shots. The cameras won't focus closer than about four feet, so the fish will look much smaller than you remember them. These cameras work best when it's sunny with good visibility and the subject fish as close as the camera allows.

They do work OK above the water too, so make a great knock-around camera to haul around wet or dry without paranoia about theft, saltwater or damage. Try a picture of the beautiful mountains of Kaua'i as you float in the waters of Hanalei Bay.

Po'ipu Area

Po'ipu is the most popular vacation spot in Kaua'i. People go for the sun, (less than twenty inches of rain a year), warm weather, a large assortment of accommodations, golf, and plenty of restaurants. Large hotels offer luxurious rooms, water slides and other amenities of the total destination. Inexpensive condos can be found, some even have an ocean view. Houses for rent are also common here, so you'll have plenty of choices.

While the majority of folks hang out at their resort pool or beach, there are some excellent snorkeling sites too. Some of the beaches are protected by outer reef, and some are protected from southern swell by their angle and offshore reefs. When south swell picks up (most often in the summer), you do have some choices here in case a given beach is too rough.

In many ways, safe snorkeling is easier to find than good swimming because most of the beaches have somewhat shallow reefs. The big hotel beaches (such as the Sheraton) usually have good swimming, but less well-known snorkeling sites (such as Koloa Landing and Ho'ai Bay) will often be calmer.

For excursions, the town of Hanapepe is only a half-hour drive west, where you'll find boats leaving from Port Allen.

Of special interest in the south are the Maha'ulepu beaches (our first four sites). All are along the coast between Po'ipu and the lovely Ha'upu mountain range. Roads may change in the future, but for now, entry is through dirt roads across what used to be cane fields. The sugar cane is gone since it's no longer profitable, so various experimental fields are now in use. Po'ipu itself may eventually encroach on this lovely area.

The further east you head from Po'ipu through the Maha'ulepu area, the more wind-swept the beaches are. Watch the form of the trees – if most of the trees are bent over at a 45 degree angle, it's probably a windy spot!

The south has plenty to offer most of the year with popular public beaches, wide sand hotel beaches, secluded snorkeling sites, and unexpectedly good snorkeling at numerous little bays.

We'll start at the northeastern end when describing these sites – continuing with our clockwise listing.

118

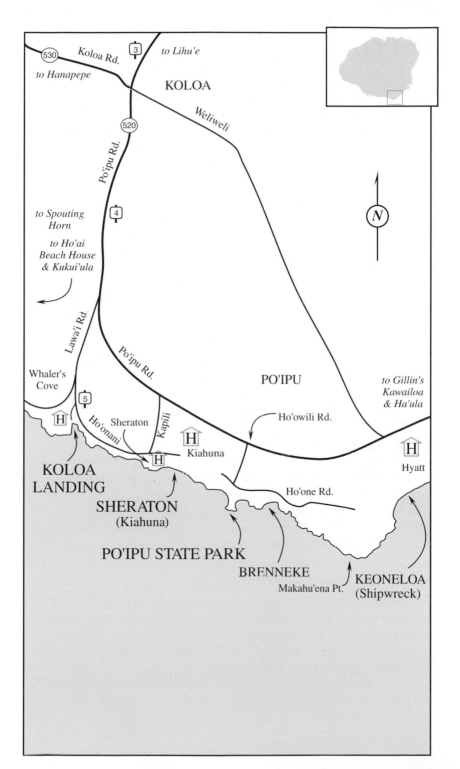

to Lihu'e

Koloa Rd.

530

to Hanapepe

KOLOA

3

520

Weliweli

Po'ipu Rd.

4

to Spouting
Horn

to Ho'ai
Beach House
& Kukui'ula

N

Lawa'i Rd.

Whaler's
Cove

Po'ipu Rd.

PO'IPU

to Gillin's
Kawailoa
& Ha'ula

5

H

Ho'onani

Sheraton

Kapili

Ho'owili Rd.

H

Kiahuna

H

Hyatt

KOLOA
LANDING

Ho'one Rd.

SHERATON
(Kiahuna)

PO'IPU STATE PARK

BRENNEKE

Makahu'ena Pt.

KEONELOA
(Shipwreck)

Kipu Kai

Access to Kipu Kai beaches is, for the time being, by boat only since the single road across the Ha'upu Mountains is private. There are actually four beaches at privately-owned Kipu Kai, but only the longest and best one is available for public access from the water. Excursions are sometimes diverted here when waves kick up on the other side of the island. Kipu Kai is very popular with kayakers. Snorkeling is excellent if you have a chance to give it a try.

GETTING THERE   The lovely Kipu Kai area is too remote (and surrounded by mountains) for an easy hike. Instead, you'll have to snorkel here with an excursion that has permission to use one of the beaches. It's also possible to kayak when south swell is low, which is more likely in the winter or spring.

Ha'ula Beach

This windswept beach southwest of Kipu Kai can be reached by a 15-minute hike from the end of the gravel road (see map, page 121). While it's a dramatic setting, the waves are much too rough here for either safe swimming or snorkeling most of the year. The bay is tucked into the surrounding hills with sand dunes lining the back. While Ha'ula rarely provides safe water sports, it does offer excellent seclusion.

GETTING THERE   Take Po'ipu Road past the Hyatt and continue driving as the road becomes gravel. Pass the golf course and stables on your right. You'll be headed directly toward Ha'upu Mountain. At the main intersection of gravel roads, where you see the power lines, turn toward the ocean. This road is located 1.8 miles past the Hyatt. Turn right, then pass the guard shack and continue .7 of a mile (passing the quarry) until you see a parking area near the beach.

Turn left at this lot and continue driving east on the dirt road for .3 of a mile until you see Kawailoa Beach (see map, page 121), then continue driving east on the dirt road along the coast for another .3 of a mile. When you get to the end (for non-4WD vehicles anyway), park and hike in the same direction over wind-swept terrain toward the next beach. It's pretty in a stark way, but not a snorkeling destination under typical conditions.

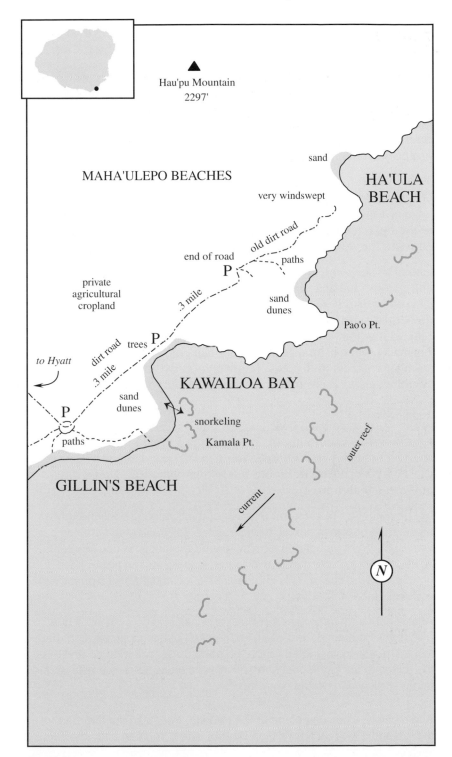

Hau'pu Mountain
2297'

MAHA'ULEPO BEACHES

sand

HA'ULA
BEACH

very windswept

old dirt road

end of road

P

paths

private
agricultural
cropland

.3 mile

sand
dunes

Pao'o Pt.

dirt road   trees   P

to Hyatt

.3 mile

KAWAILOA BAY

sand
dunes

P

snorkeling

Kamala Pt.

paths

outer reef

GILLIN'S BEACH

current

N

Kawailoa Beach

Our favorite beach in this area, Kawailoa Beach can be reached from the gravel road after it passes Gillin's Beach. It's a beautiful spot with easy access from the dirt road. The beach itself is small and picturesque – an excellent spot for a quiet picnic or some fishing. Snorkeling is best if you hike along the sand to the right to the inner protected area of a curved reef close to the shore.

While you can hike a path over the sand dunes to get here from Gillin's Beach, it's closer and easier to park in the shade along the edge of Kawailoa Bay. Snorkeling is best if you head along the sand to the right and enter the water near the curved reef that almost encloses the sandy corner.

Enter the sheltered area marked on our map (page 121) for an easy entry from sand and good protection from a reef near the shore. There is a drift here toward your right, so you might want to enter at the left (eastern) end of the reef and slowly drift to the western end. Stay well within the outer reef, snorkeling on the ocean side of the inner reef. On a calm day, beginners can enjoy this spot, but the stronger currents in this area require good swimming ability, just in case the current picks up. By all means, wear your fins.

When big south swells roll in (more often in the summer), stay out of the water at isolated beaches like this one that have minimal protection. When conditions are good, this is a great place to swim, snorkel and enjoy the solitude. You can still see damage to the reef caused by Hurricane Iniki, but the fish are plentiful. No facilities anywhere in this area.

GETTING THERE Take Po'ipu Road past the Hyatt and continue driving as the road becomes gravel, then pass the golf course and stables on your right. You'll be headed directly toward dramatic Ha'upu Mountain. At the main intersection of gravel roads, where you see power lines, turn right toward the ocean. This intersection is located 1.8 miles past the main entrance of the Hyatt.

After a right turn, pass the empty guard shack and go another .7 of a mile (past the quarry), and you'll find the first parking lot (see map, page 121). The trail to your left through the sand dunes will wind up and over the dunes to get to the best snorkeling eventually. It's a nice hike up the dunes through Christmas berry trees.

Alternatively, when you come to the parking area, take the dirt road to the left and it will reach Kawailoa Beach, where you can park just steps from the sand. This next bay is just .3 of a mile east of the parking for Gillin's Beach. We prefer this spot because it's pretty, shady and a great place to picnic. To get to the best snorkeling, simply hike back to the right along the sand. You'll be able to see the inner reef that curves out from the sand. Enter the water at the left (east) end of the inner reef since the current heads to the right. When waves pick up a bit, an outer reef offers some protection from south swells, but the offshore current is still usually fairly strong even when surf is low.

Gillin's Beach

Gillin's Beach is located near the first parking area, where you arrive at the Maha'ulepu beaches. Just a short hike from the parking area, you'll emerge from the kiawe trees to find a beautiful long almost-white sand beach. Snorkeling here is good if south swell is very low, but can be quite hazardous at other times. Waves and currents can catch you and there won't be anyone to see it happen.

This is a lovely spot to walk the long beach and picnic on the sand under the ironwoods. Listen for the pleasant birdsongs and flashes of colorful birds.. No facilities here and few people.

This same parking lot has a path to the left that will eventually lead to the safest snorkeling spot (between Gillin's and Kawailoa). There's plenty of reef along Gillin's Beach, but it's shallow, with rocky and difficult access. Begin at the easiest access, then experts can explore further afield.

GETTING THERE From Po'ipu, head toward the Hyatt, passing the hotel, then the golf course, then the stables – all on your right. The road is now gravel, but wide and heads directly toward Ha'upu Mountain rising almost straight up 2,297 feet.

At 1.8 miles past the Hyatt, you'll come to a "major" intersection with power poles (not telephone poles as they're usually described). Take a right turn here, pass the empty guard shack and head .7 of a mile to the sand dunes parking area. You'll pass a quarry on your right.

This first parking area (see map, page 121) has two roads leading in either direction as well as two paths closer to the middle of the parking circle. The path (not the road) to the right leads about 75 yards through the kiawe trees to Gillin's Beach, where you'll find a beautiful long beach lined with ironwoods and trees full of birds. You may hike a mile on sand in either direction and not see a single person.

Keoneloa Beach (Shipwreck)

This pretty beach in front of the Hyatt is nice for a stroll and tanning. It tends to be rougher than others in the Po'ipu area, so isn't the best bet for snorkeling or swimming. If you happen to catch it on a very calm day, snorkel along the cliffs at the left end of the beach. Leave jumping off the cliffs to the locals and guys who still feel a need to either prove their manhood or lose it. There is some public parking at the eastern end of the beach.

GETTING THERE Take Poipu Road east past the Hyatt. Then take Ainako Road toward the beach. You'll find a parking lot with public access, showers, and restrooms, but not the safest swimming or snorkeling, especially when south swells arrive in the summer.

Brennecke Beach

Brennecke, although next door to Po'ipu Beach Park, is definitely NOT a snorkeling beach. You might want to pause and watch the body-surfing. Brennecke seems to catch all the waves from the south and sand drops off quickly forming a strong undertow.

GETTING THERE Brennecke is the first beach to the east of the Po'ipu Beaches (see map, page 127), located along Ho'one Road just to the east of Po'ipu Beach Park. Parking is scarce near Brennecke, but you'll find a large parking lot across the street from Po'ipu Beach Park.

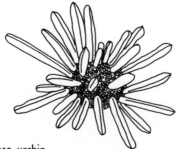

slatepencil sea urchin

Discounts

Discounts are available for many excursions. If you're so inclined, a little work and the right questions can save you a fair chunk of change. Begin by picking up one of the numerous free promotional magazines such as Kaua'i Gold. These are readily available at the airport, hotels and shops. They usually include special offers, coupons and other deals to attract customers.

Calling an excursion office and asking if there are any special offers can sometimes pay off, especially when tourism is slower. Summer and holidays the ships fill more quickly, but there is still plenty of competition on Kaua'i, so it's always worth a try.

Ships often charge less for children and nothing for toddlers. Each ship has its own definition of child and adult. Don't hesitate to ask about senior discounts, repeat customer discounts, and kama'aina rate (if you live in the islands and can prove it by showing your driver's license). Sometimes discounts are provided to AAA members.

For discounts ranging from 10-20%, try Activity Warehouse:

Kapa'a (808) 742-2300

Princeville (808) 826-4100

travelhawaii.com

It helps to have a flexible schedule and be able to go at the last minute.

For a free trip, sign up for a timeshare offer. You will have to sit through an hour or two of sales talk in exchange for your bargain trip. Do not underestimate their sales ability!

When you do book tickets ahead of time and charge them to your credit card, remember that when the ship goes out with or without you, you will be charged for the trip. The fine print usually requires you to cancel at least 24 hours ahead. You may wake up to weather that doesn't suit you only to find that the ship sailed anyway, and you will get to pay as agreed. Also, your destination isn't guaranteed. You might have your heart set on Lehua Island only to find the ship change to Kipu Kai due to rough weather in the channel. This does not entitle you to cancel. Keep in mind they must make changes for safety reasons, so go with the flow and trust your captain.

Po'ipu Beach Park

Located in the center of the Po'ipu area, this popular beach is better for snorkeling than swimming. The distinctive spit of sand connecting the shore to the rocky area offshore is one of the few examples in Hawai'i of a tambolo (see page 127.) This division creates two separate back-to-back beaches. Snorkel to the right (west) anywhere within the area protected by offshore reefs. The beach to the left is equally good when swells are similar. Pick the day's calmest side.

While the beach itself is smooth sand, the underwater area is strewn with large boulders making you vulnerable if sudden waves are high enough to cross the offshore reefs. Take a good look at conditions before you enter the water and inquire at the lifeguard station if you have any doubts. Just because lots of people swim here, doesn't mean it's entirely safe for either swimming or snorkeling. As long as waves stop at the outer reef, it's all very easy, but sudden waves can and do cross the reef. This happens when waves roll in from storms in the Southern Pacific.

Snorkeling here is not as good as it was before Hurricane Iniki and you'll see some of the damage to the reef. At least the junk (like sewing machines) has been removed by now. Still, it's a lovely beach with all facilities and you're certain to see some fish. Showers, restrooms, covered picnic areas and lifeguard are available. It's a nice place to hang out on sand or grass with some shade under scattered palms. Although popular, there's usually ample parking available in the large dirt lot mauka (toward the mountains). People come and go frequently, so wait a bit if necessary and you'll certainly find a spot to park.

Snorkeling is in three to fifteen foot deep water where you can explore around amid the boulder habitat while being careful to stay within the protected area.

GETTING THERE Po'ipu Beach Park is located next to the corner of Ho'one Road and Ho'owili Road on the beach side of the town of Po'ipu. Park in the large gravel lot on the corner (see map, page 127) or along the side of the road where legal.

In case you're confused: the beach in front of the Sheraton is sometimes called Po'ipu Beach, while Po'ipu Beach Park is the one with a tambolo in the center.

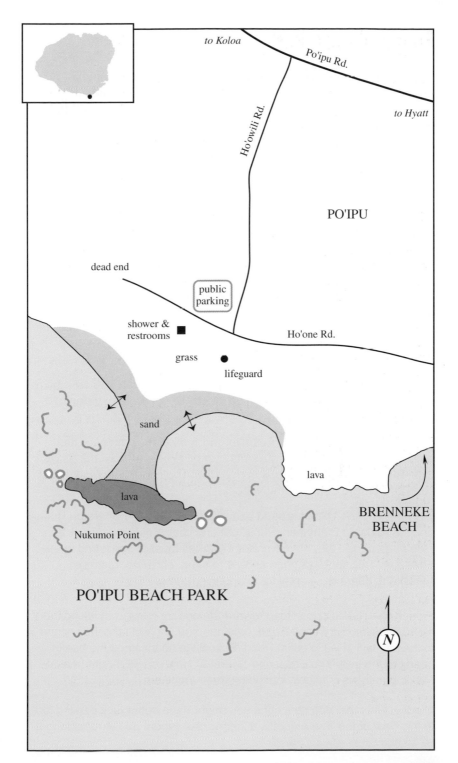

to Koloa

Po'ipu Rd.

Ho'owili Rd.

to Hyatt

PO'IPU

dead end

public parking

shower & restrooms

Ho'one Rd.

grass

lifeguard

sand

lava

BRENNEKE BEACH

lava

Nukumoi Point

PO'IPU BEACH PARK

N

Kiahuna — Sheraton Beach (Po'ipu Beach)

This long beautiful curve of sand stretches from the Kiahuna Plantation to the Sheraton Hotel. It's also called Po'ipu Beach, which can be confused with nearby Po'ipu Beach Park. Parking and public access are provided, but the best spots are difficult to find. Check our map (page 129) to find the more convenient spots close to the best snorkeling otherwise you may have to hike the length of the beach, or more.

For snorkeling, enter from the sand at the eastern end of the Sheraton and snorkel in the most protected area. Watch the waves closely because waves are somewhat, but not entirely, caught by the offshore reef. Entry is usually easy from the sandy beach, although there are some rocks to watch for. Of course, snorkelers can see them more easily than swimmers. Since the beach slope is rather sudden, be alert for a surprisingly strong undertow. Swimming is also good, especially on calm days. Out a bit you'll see mostly rubble with some small lobe and encrusting coral heads in 5-10' depth. There's plenty of room to explore, but don't wander out into the great surfing territory.

This reef was damaged by Hurricane Iniki, but you'll still find plenty of interesting fish, such as tangs, boxfish, needlefish, colorful wrasses and large cornetfish.

Kiahuna Beach is well worth a trip and a nice spot to enjoy the beach with showers and restrooms handy. Pretty as it is, the waves can still pick up when storms arrive from the south, so check it out carefully before entering the water.

GETTING THERE This long sand beach is shared by the Sheraton Hotel and the Kiahuna Plantation. Public parking is available in several spots (see map, page 129), but we prefer the small lot at the east end of the Sheraton. This spot has good access to sand, showers, restrooms, grass, and offers easy entry for snorkeling or swimming.

From Koloa, take Po'ipu Road toward the ocean. Instead of taking the Y to the left, which is Po'ipu Road, continue straight and take the second Y to the left, which is Ho'onani Road. Follow Ho'onani along the beach nearly to the end. You'll pass the Sheraton Hotel on your right (makai). Public parking is available in at least three locations.

Midday, when parking gets tight, you might have better luck parking just to the west of the Sheraton. It's a longer hike (about 300 yards) along a

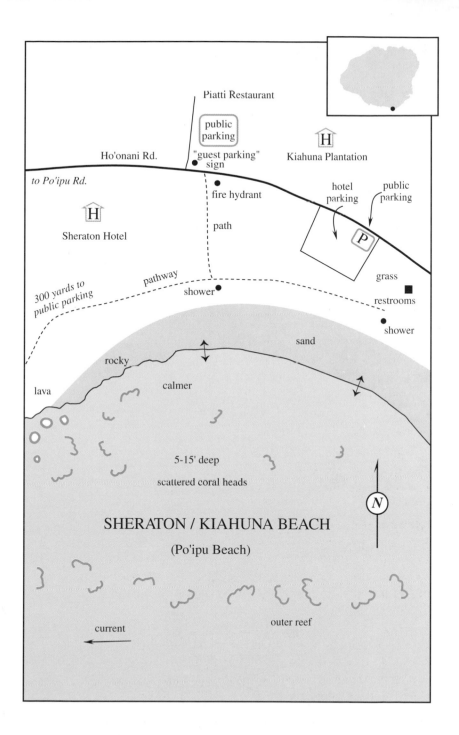

Piatti Restaurant

public parking

Ho'onani Rd.

"guest parking" sign

H Kiahuna Plantation

to Po'ipu Rd.

fire hydrant

hotel parking

public parking

H

path

Sheraton Hotel

P

pathway

grass

300 yards to public parking

shower

restrooms

shower

sand

rocky

calmer

lava

5-15' deep

scattered coral heads

N

SHERATON / KIAHUNA BEACH

(Po'ipu Beach)

outer reef

current

concrete path that traverses the entire front of the hotel. There are twenty one parking spaces here with a shower at the far west end of the lot.

Toward the middle of the Sheraton, there's more hidden "guest parking" in the shaded lot mauka of the Sheraton. The sign says "guest parking for Piatti Restaurant, Kiahuna Plantation, and day beach access only." It's directly across Ho'onani Road from the fire hydrant. From here you'll find a path through the Sheraton grounds to the west end of the beach.

Beyond the east end of the Sheraton, you'll find the last and best parking lot with beach access parking. This spot gets you within twenty yards of the beach, where you can enter for good snorkeling or swimming. Restrooms are located across the grass to the east and a public shower is found toward the beach.

pyramid butterflyfish

I Like to Watch

"For some reason, the barracuda don't seem scary, any more than the ray does. For some reason, none of this seems scary. Even the idea of maybe encountering a smallish s___k doesn't seem altogether bad.

It's beginning to dawn on me that all the fish and eels and crabs and shrimps and plankton who live and work down here are just too busy to be thinking about me.

I'm a traveller from another dimension, not really a part of their already event-filled world, not programmed one way or another–food or yikes–into their instinct circuits. They have important matters to attend to, and they don't care whether I watch or not. And so I watch."

–Dave Barry

Koloa Landing

Popular with kayakers and divers, this site doesn't look like much and has no facilities other than the boat ramp and a dozen parking spaces. Yet it offers surprisingly calm water with great snorkeling. Koloa Landing is hidden from view, so check our map (page 133) or you may miss it.

Entry is easy in the boat ramp with its gentle ramp. Just walk right into the channel taking care not to slip on the wet ramp. Watch the small swell as you enter, but there's good clearance in the center (at least three feet). Snorkel anywhere – left, right and straight in front. There's lots to see very close to shore and the bay is well-protected from the bigger waves offshore. Depth ranges from five to twenty feet close to shore, dropping deeper as you get out to sea.

We enjoyed an evening snorkel here when most of the south had big swells and poor visibility. At Koloa Landing we saw turtles in the deeper areas, huge parrotfish, schools of tangs so thick you couldn't see through them, Moorish idols, trumpetfish, and pairs of butterfly-fish – teardrop, longnose, blue-striped, and multiband. And we had the little bay entirely to ourselves.

The short, steep dirt road that ducks down to Koloa Landing is bumpy enough that you might hesitate to drive down in a rental car or anytime after a heavy rain. If you're adventurous and good at dodging deep ruts, you can drive right on down and park.

GETTING THERE   From the town of Koloa, head south toward the water on Po'ipu Road. Instead of taking the Y to the left which continues to be Po'ipu Road, go straight toward the water. Stay left at the Y where a right would lead to Spouting Horn. The left side of the Y is Ho'onani Road. Watch carefully and you'll immediately see a rough dirt road that drops steeply down to Koloa Landing (see map, page 133).

The road is pitted, so you might prefer to park elsewhere and walk. You'll be able to see that it's a short walk, only about 100 yards. Koloa Landing is located right at mile marker 5 and looks more like a driveway than a road. It has space below for about a dozen cars, but no facilities or sand.

Enter Hanaka'ape Bay straight through the boat channel in the center, where it's usually very calm.

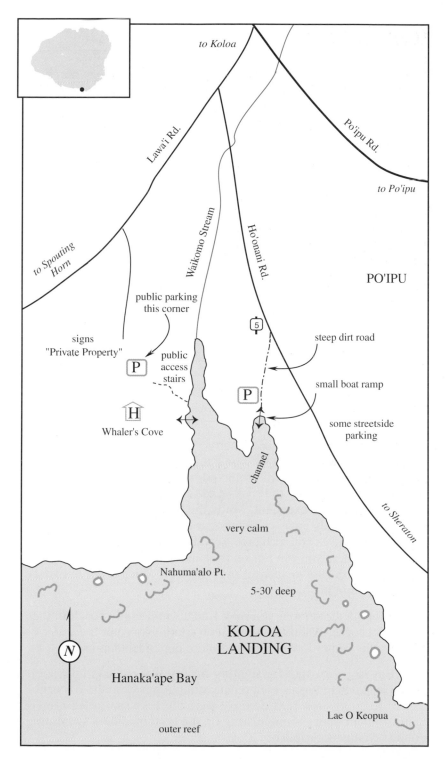

to Koloa

Lawa'i Rd.

Po'ipu Rd.

to Po'ipu

to Spouting Horn

Waikomo Stream

Ho'onani Rd.

PO'IPU

public parking
this corner

5

steep dirt road

signs
"Private Property"

P

public
access
stairs

P

small boat ramp

H

Whaler's Cove

some streetside
parking

channel

to Sheraton

very calm

Nahuma'alo Pt.

5-30' deep

N

KOLOA
LANDING

Hanaka'ape Bay

Lae O Keopua

outer reef

133

Hanaka'ape Bay (Whaler's Cove)

The Whaler's Cove lot provides designated public parking spaces, although the signs at the entrance give no hint that the public is welcome. From inside the lot (to the left) you will see beach access signs leading to a short hike down stairs. You'll have to enter from the river here in order to snorkel out into Hanaka'ape Bay, so might prefer high tide. It's also a bit rockier here, so our preference is to enter from the Koloa Landing boat ramp. Either way you will find a good snorkeling destination in calm Hanaka'ape Bay.

GETTING THERE   From the town of Koloa, take Po'ipu Road toward the beach. Instead of taking the Y to the left for Po'ipu, continue and follow the Y (Lawa'i Road) to the right toward Spouting Horn (see map, page 133). Immediately turn left into the Whaler's Cove parking lot on your left in spite of the warning signs. You'll find the marked public parking and access path at the far left of the lot (see map, page 135). The steps will drop you down at the west side of the river. High tide is better here if you want the easiest entry. Most people would prefer the ease and comfort of the boat ramp, especially if they don't wear booties. The entry at Whaler's Cove is rocky, with no sand or any facilities.

Ho'ai Bay (Prince Kuhio)

Although the Prince Kuhio Park across the street from this bay is not open to the general public, you can park along the street to snorkel in this small, mostly-protected bay. This isn't a great swimming spot because of all the rocks and the shallowness near shore, but the snorkeling is excellent. Study the bay for a bit and you'll find a narrow sandy entry channel near the center. It's only about a foot wide, but gives you a chance to walk in to a larger sand-bottomed area where you can put on fins and adjust your mask at your leisure. Then it's easy to snorkel over the reef, which is ten to twenty feet deep within the bay.

Depending on the season, you may find a small sandy beach in the right-hand corner Although we've seen snorkelers enter the water on the right, the center looks safer and more dependable to us.

Ho'ai Bay is a great spot for sighting turtles. We've marked the spot on our map where turtles congregate straight out from the eastern edge of Kuhio Shores. Last time we were there we saw at least ten of them from one spot – some resting on the bottom, others swimming around, eyeing us curiously.

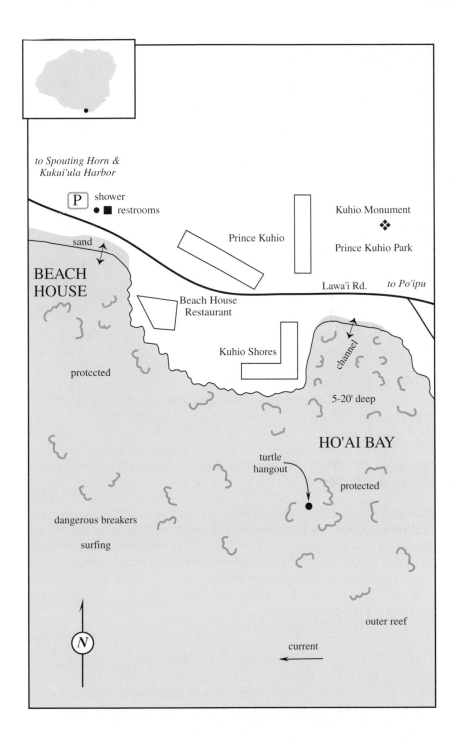

to Spouting Horn &
Kukui'ula Harbor

P shower
● ■ restrooms

sand

BEACH
HOUSE

Prince Kuhio

Kuhio Monument
❖

Prince Kuhio Park

Lawa'i Rd.   to Po'ipu

Beach House
Restaurant

Kuhio Shores

channel

protected

5-20' deep

HO'AI BAY

turtle
hangout

protected

dangerous breakers

surfing

outer reef

N

current

Coral isn't too exciting here, but we found a great variety of fish: lots of orangeband surgeonfish and yellow tangs, schools of Moorish idols, parrotfish, pairs of butterflyfish (threadfin, fourspot, ornate), and a spotted eagle ray hanging out not far from the turtles.

Don't get tempted to snorkel around the point to Beach House because it's rougher off the point and not deep enough to provide good clearance should a bigger wave sweep in. Leave that area to the surfers. Watch the current here too because it tends to pull you toward the west.

We've seen lots of people have unnecessary trouble walking in or out of Ho'ai Bay. Any site like this with a narrow entry and rocks to fall on can be a challenge if done the wrong way. Walking in or out with fins on can be hazardous. Simply keep fins in hand, walk slowly out to the sandy spot beyond the swell, then don your fins and you're all set. Exit the same way, so that you don't risk being knocked on the rocks by an unexpected wave.

GETTING THERE   Heading south from Koloa, take Po'ipu Road toward the ocean. Rather than turning left toward Po'ipu, continue and take the Y to the right which is marked "Spouting Horn." This is Lawa'i Road, where you will drive directly to Ho'ai Bay (see map, page 135). Parking is usually available along the road here, but you might have to park further west toward the Beach House restaurant on a weekend.

Prince Kuhio Park is directly across the street (mauka), but is not open for general use. The condos at the far western end of the beach are called Kuhio Shores.

Park along the road next to Ho'ia Bay or further up Lawa'i Road near the Beach House restaurant, where you will find more parking, plus restrooms and a shower. Ho'ia Bay is right next to the road, so you can see the little patches of sand as well as the small channel near the center. Access is easiest from the center.

Beach House (Lawa'i Beach)

This bay in front of the Beach House restaurant on the way to Spouting Horn has excellent snorkeling with easy entry from the sand. There's a parking lot with shower and restrooms right across the street as well as more parking along Lawa'i Road. The beach itself is sometimes called Lawa'i and also often confused with Ho'ai Bay a short walk to the east.

This is a small bay so come in the early morning or late afternoon if you want to avoid the crowds. Surfers will be catching waves further out, but the inner area is well-protected. You'll have to watch out for a drift to the right that is stronger when those surfers are getting good waves.

Lawa'i has an excellent variety of fish and some healthy coral patches, all quite near shore in about 5-15' of water. The water isn't terrifically clear when south swells are arriving, but you can get quite close to the fish here and get a good look anyway.

If you want to see turtles and don't find them here, just walk on down to Ho'ai Bay on the other side of the restaurant and Kuhio Shores, where they're abundant.

These two beaches offer similar conditions, but the entry at Beach House is a bit easier for a beginner since there's more sand. Both beaches often have a slow current that tends to pull you to the right (west), so inexperienced snorkelers need to look up now and then to avoid trouble. By all means, stay out of the surfing area. The sand level will vary with the seasons, but Beach House tends to have quite a bit more than nearby Ho'ai Bay.

GETTING THERE Heading south from the town of Koloa, take Po'ipu Road toward the ocean. Instead of taking a Y toward Po'ipu, continue and watch for the Y on Lawa'i Road that leads to the right toward Spouting Horn. You'll pass the small Ho'ai Bay, then Kuhio Shores and Prince Kuhio condos. Just past the Beach House restaurant, you'll see the beach (see map, page 135). Parking, restrooms and shower are all located directly across Lawa'i Road. There is also some parking along the side of Lawa'i Road.

Kukui'ula Bay

Located just to the east of Spouting Horn, you'll find the Kukui'ula small boat harbor. It's well-protected, with a reef that offers unusually calm conditions for swimming or snorkeling. The breakwater at the eastern end (to the left) provides good snorkeling with good visibility. Amenities include restrooms, showers, picnic tables and plenty of parking.

GETTING THERE Head west on Lawa'i Road passing Ho'ai Bay and Beach House. You will see the harbor off to your left (makai) just before you get to Spouting Horn (see map, page 119). From Lawa'i Road, take either 'Alani'o or 'Amio toward the water. This will bring you to the eastern end of the bay, where the harbor is located.

Southwest Area

While the southwest of Kaua'i offers an abundance of sand, it also has some of the most hazardous swimming conditions, with heavy currents offshore. This is surfing territory, so seldom offers safe swimming or snorkeling. There are exceptions, such as Salt Pond Beach, where you will find a natural lava breakwater that normally provides safe snorkeling. Most of the southwestern beaches serve better as spots to walk in solitude along pristine sands stretching off as far as you can see, with no one in sight.

Wahiawa Bay (Ahulua Bay)

This sandy beach, with cliffs along both sides, offers protection from both winds and currents. Heavy runoff from the river can make the water murky, but snorkeling can be good when there's little rain.

Public access is unavailable at this time, but dirt roads run across the fields makai of the highway just west of Numila.

Glass Beach

While not a snorkeling or swimming destination, this little beach is made up of well-worn pieces of glass. It's a tiny beach just east of Port Allen.

GETTING THERE   From Lihu'e, take Highway 50 west to Hanapepe. Then head for Port Allen before crossing the Hanapepe River. This little beach is to the east of the port.

Hanapepe Beach Park

Located near the mouth of the Hanapepe River, this beach gets too much silt to offer good snorkeling. It does have restrooms, showers, and parking.

GETTING THERE   From Lihu'e, as you approach Hanapepe on Highway 50, this park is located on the eastern corner of Hanapepe Bay (see map, page 139). This is near Kaua'i's largest harbor on this side of the island. Excursions depart here from Port Allen Harbor to the Na Pali coast and Lehua Island.

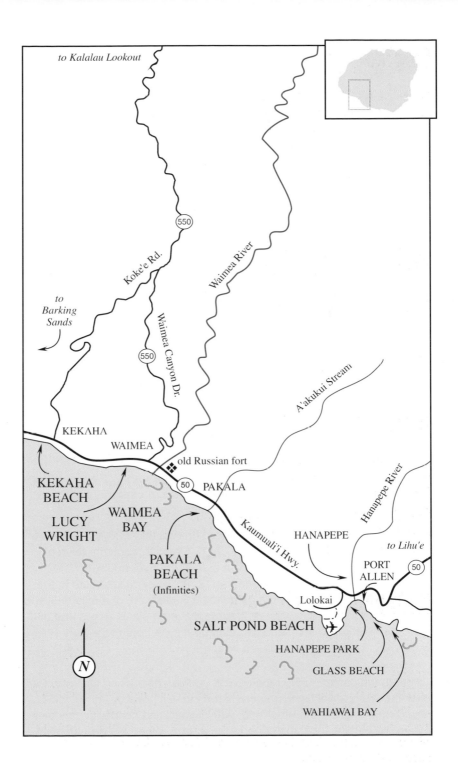

to Kalalau Lookout

550

Koke'e Rd.

Waimea River

to
Barking
Sands

Waimea Canyon Dr.

550

A'akukui Stream

KEKΛHΛ

WAIMEA

old Russian fort

Hanapepe River

KEKAHA
BEACH

50   PAKALA

LUCY
WRIGHT

WAIMEA
BAY

Kaumuali'i Hwy.

HANAPEPE

to Lihu'e

PAKALA
BEACH
(Infinities)

PORT
ALLEN

50

Lolokai

SALT POND BEACH

HANAPEPE PARK

GLASS BEACH

N

WAHIAWAI BAY

139

Salt Pond Beach Park

An outer reef as well as a natural lava breakwater nearly fully protect this sand beach. It's a great place to go when swells kick in from the south. The lava wall only protects the two ends of the beach, so small swells can still enter in the middle. Stick close to either end if in doubt about the swells or current.

You'll find plenty of parking, showers, restrooms, large covered picnic areas, grass, sand and shade. The wide beach is mostly sandy with some rocks, but just deep enough for swimming. Snorkeling is excellent with a variety of large fish near shore. With the easy entry and 5-10' depth, it's just like a salt water swimming pool. Because of the gap in the lava at the center of the beach, there can be a current, so you should still use fins and watch children carefully, especially if you see any sign of swells.

Snorkeling is best at either end, but there is also a shallower completely enclosed pool beyond the far southeastern end of the beach. You can often watch ultralights take off from the adjacent airstrip. The dirt road at this end of the bay can be muddy after a heavy rain, so you might want to park in the lot and walk the short way to the water rather than risk getting your rental car stuck in the mud.

While Salt Pond isn't the prettiest beach in Kaua'i, it is certainly one of the safest and easiest, so we recommend it for beginners. More advanced snorkelers will enjoy occasional large fish wandering in from deeper water. A popular family spot used mostly by local folks. On a very calm day, experienced snorkelers can explore out beyond the protection of the lava walls.

GETTING THERE   From Lihu'e, head west on Highway 530, then continue west on Highway 50 (see map, page 141). Cross through the town of Hanapepe (Port Allen) to the western side of the river and watch for signs to Salt Pond Park at mile marker 17. At the sign, take Lele to the left. After .3 of a mile, turn right on Lokokai Road for .6 of a mile until you see the park with its showers, restrooms, covered picnic tables and plenty of space on grass and sand. Snorkel directly in front of the park (the western end of the semi-enclosed beach).

To get to the eastern end of the beach, you can hike along the sand to your left. Alternatively, you can cross the old salt pond by car on the paved road to get to the other end, where you'll find no facilities other than a dirt parking lot at the edge of the airport. When the ground is dry, you can drive right up to the beach. When muddy, you'll want to park back in the lot, where the ground is more level.

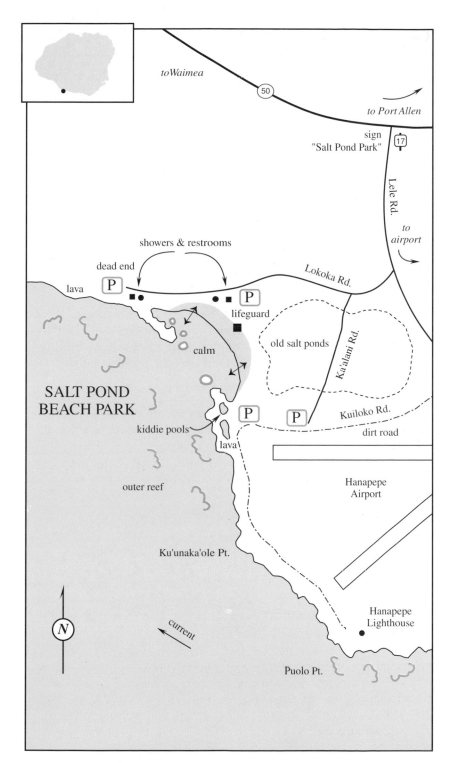

to Waimea

50

to Port Allen

sign
"Salt Pond Park"

17

Lele Rd.

to
airport

showers & restrooms

dead end

lava

P

Lokoka Rd.

P

lifeguard

old salt ponds

Ka'alani Rd.

calm

SALT POND
BEACH PARK

kiddie pools

lava

P

P

Kuiloko Rd.

dirt road

outer reef

Hanapepe
Airport

Ku'unaka'ole Pt.

Hanapepe
Lighthouse

N

current

Puolo Pt.

Pakala Beach (Infinities)

Pakala is a very popular surfing area, dubbed Infinities for the long waves that roll along the edge. When the inner shallow reef area is calm, it has OK snorkeling, but there's always some current making it advisable only for advanced snorkelers.

When surf's up (especially in the summer), the water won't be very clear anyway, even if it's calmer near shore.

GETTING THERE   On Highway 50, between Waimea and Hanapepe (see map, page 139), you'll find the little town of Pakala with beach along the south side of town. Public access is near the bridge. Park on either side of the road and take the unmarked path about 150 yards to the beach.

Lucy Wright Beach Park

Lucy Wright Beach Park isn't the best spot to snorkel due to the river run-off. While it provides good swimming in calm water, visibility tends to be very poor. The beach itself isn't the prettiest either.

It's does have restrooms, showers and convenient parking.

GETTING THERE   Heading west on Highway 50, drive to the town of Waimea and cross the river. Here, head toward the beach to arrive at the park (see map, page 139).

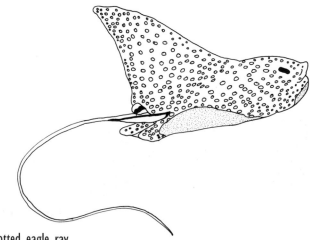

spotted eagle ray

If You Love the Reef

- Show respect for the reef creatures by causing them no harm.

- Avoid touching the coral, as touching kills it.

- Come as a respectful visitor rather than as a predator.

- Leave the many beautiful creatures you find there in peace so that others may enjoy them as you have.

- Allow the fish their usual diet rather than feeding them. Feeding them ultimately destroys their natural balance, and causes their numbers to decline.

- Think of the creatures of the reef as fellow travelers in our life journey and then you may comprehend their magnificence.

- Join our reef easter egg hunt: try to find and dive for at least one piece of trash on every snorkel, and take it away with you. It sharpens your eye, and if enough folks do it, it will be hard to find any. Don't try to clean up the whole world. Just pick up one or two things every time you're out.

- Use sunscreen less, and cover-ups more. Sunscreen dissolves in the water, and is toxic to fish and coral. A lycra body suit or a wetsuit takes care of most of your body better anyway. Save your sunscreen for your sensitive face.

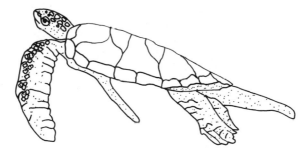

green sea turtle

West Area

The far western area of Kaua'i has a fifteen-mile long sandy beach, but rarely offers safe snorkeling or swimming. The prevailing currents wrapping around Kaua'i come together offshore here to create some unusually strong and unpredictable currents.

Come for the beauty, the wide empty beaches, the warm dry weather and the view of Ni'ihau Island at sunset. If you're getting way too much rain elsewhere on Kaua'i, you may find this corner of the island dry and appealing.

The only disadvantage is how long it can take to get to the further locations, as the roads gradually get worse. Those who drive out here consider that just part of the adventure, and one way to leave the crowds behind.

You won't find accommodations, golf courses, or shopping in the west, just endless sand dunes all the way to the sharp cliffs of the Na Pali coast. A few little towns along Highway 50 do offer food and gas for the journey.

Kekaha Beach Park

This is a lovely long beach, but it tends to have heavy surf. It's best to leave this one to the locals unless you get lucky and hit very calm conditions in the winter. It does have good snorkeling and swimming when unusually calm, but you'll need to pay close attention to currents and swells.

Facilities are located across the road from the center of the beach. You'll find a lifeguard station at the west end of the narrow park, with low sand dunes between the highway and the ocean. There is little or no shade along the beach, but it does have a good view of Ni'ihau in the distance.

GETTING THERE   Along Highway 50 to the west of the town of Waimea, you'll find this long stretch of beach on the ocean side (makai) of the highway (see map, page 145). There's plenty of sand and facilities near the lifeguard station, although the lifeguard looked rather lonely when we were last there, since the beach in front was utterly empty. Surfers will be well offshore when waves are good. If you're considering swimming or snorkeling here, stop by and check with the lifeguard about currents and swells. The current here usually sweeps west at a good clip.

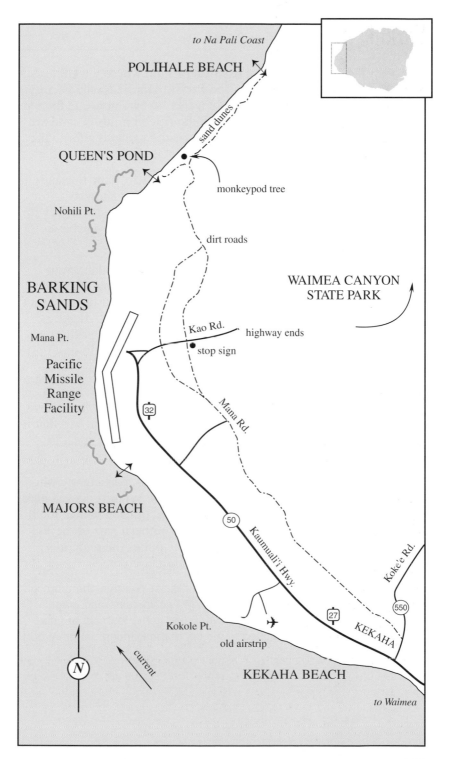

to Na Pali Coast

POLIHALE BEACH

sand dunes

QUEEN'S POND

monkeypod tree

Nohili Pt.

dirt roads

WAIMEA CANYON
STATE PARK

BARKING
SANDS

Mana Pt.

Kao Rd.

highway ends

stop sign

Pacific
Missile
Range
Facility

32

Mana Rd.

50

Kaumuali'i Hwy.

MAJORS BEACH

Koke'e Rd.

550

27

KEKAHA

Kokole Pt.

old airstrip

N

current

KEKAHA BEACH

to Waimea

Barking Sands (Majors Beach)

Barking Sands refers to a great expanse of sand where the US tests some of its missiles. Surprisingly, the Pacific Missile Range Facility welcomes visitors and even throws in a free "show" now and then as they lob missile into the sea. Although the fifteen miles of sand are all part of Barking Sands, some people use the name to refer to the Missile Facility area.

Just drive up to the gate and ask to go to the beach. They'll usually direct you to nearby Majors Beach. Here you'll find showers, restrooms, some shade and plenty of sand with low dunes. If any of you are in the military, they even have simple houses available to rent at a remarkably low price.

Typically the waves are kicking up making this a long dangerous beach complete with strong currents and undertow. You might be lucky and find it flat enough to snorkel. One of the reasons this spot is so dangerous is that the open-ocean currents divide to flow around Kaua'i, but come together again in the seas off Barking Sands to create some very rough and unpredictable conditions.

Barking Sands is a nice place to watch the sunset over Ni'ihau. As for the barking sands, we've read the various theories, but haven't yet heard any barking. Supposedly, the sand contains tiny holes that resonate when rubbed together briskly. Perhaps our problem was that it was VERY hot here and so we didn't try hard enough. Expect to need shoes to walk on this hot sand if you arrive midday.

You'll note that Kaua'i had an abundance of sand, particularly when compared to the other major Hawai'ian islands. What is doesn't have is the variety of sand colors: black, red, green, or even white. You'll find the more colorful sands mostly in the southern part of the Big Island, where more recent volcanic action supplies the materials. Kaua'i's beaches are all nearly identical caramel-colored.

GETTING THERE Take Highway 50 west well past Waimea, then turn left at the entrance to the Pacific Missile Range Facility (see map, page 145). Ask for directions to the beach when you come to the guard station. The park-like area is located to the left of the Barking Sands Airport.

Queen's Pond

Not really worth a trip for snorkeling. Queen's Pond is just a varying size area of shallow water just inland from the breakers in the middle of a huge beach lined with sand dunes. This spot is hot, bare and beautiful in its own way, but has no facilities. The pond is sometimes too shallow to do anything except wade. It also requires a long hike over hot sand. By 9 a.m. it can be too hot to walk barefooted.

You may see 4WD vehicles down on the sand, but rental cars could very well get stuck and require a VERY expensive tow. See our map for where to park and hike if you want to check out Queen's Pond.

GETTING THERE As you head west on Highway 50 (see map, page 145), the highway eventually takes you to the Pacific Missile Range Facility. At the entrance, jog to the right on Kao Road, then left, with signs marking the way on a dirt road to Polihale State Park. When this dirt road heads straight for the high dunes, you'll come to a huge monkeypod tree (3.3 miles from the end of the highway), where the road along the dunes splits in two directions. This is the only large tree in the area, so you can't miss it.

At the tree, go left for Queen's Pond and drive as far as seems prudent (only about .1 of a mile). Park along the road and walk over the sandiest stretch at the end. Follow any path up and over the tall dunes to your right for about 200 yards and you'll emerge on the vast sand beach.

While sands shift in the dunes, water is rearranging the sands under the sea. It's typical for the bottom to change here with the seasons. Sometimes there's be a long sandbar offshore, creating its own currents and dangers. The Pond itself will also be affected by changing sands.

Moorish idol

Polihale State Park

This long stretch of sandy beach lined by hundred-foot tall sand dunes is located beyond the far western end of the highway. The park, at the edge of the Na Pali coast, is as far as you can go by car – or foot for that matter. It's hot here mid-days and afternoons, dry and rather stark. The park at the end of the dirt road does offer showers, restrooms, picnic tables, and even some shade. This is a great place to watch the sunset over Ni'ihau. When water is calm enough, snorkeling is OK at best, especially to the west beyond the end of the sand. Be cautious about conditions before going in.

This is one of the less hazardous stretches along the fifteen-mile long beach that wraps Kaua'i's western side. Be absolutely sure the current isn't too strong before venturing out in the water here since there may not be anyone around to rescue you if you should get swept away. The current flows to your left rather than toward the Na Pali coast, which is certainly a plus. As always, don't go in the water without your fins!

Polihale State Park is about five miles beyond the end of the highway and the dirt road is quite slow, so allow extra time if you want to drive all this way. If you plan to stay till dark, make sure that you memorize the road carefully as you arrive, because a moonless night can make the dirt road hard to see and you won't want to be lost on any of the side roads.

Come prepared for heat and sun. This is the hot, dry corner of Kaua'i at the end of fifteen miles of sand. Most of the natural water has long since been diverted for use in the sugar cane fields. Though sugar cane is gradually being replaced, water is most unlikely to be returned. Bring plenty of your own.

If you're in Po'ipu during the summer, looking for a day's drive to the end of the road, you might want to consider Ke'e Beach in the north instead. It's prettier and may not take any longer (depending on traffic). Besides, good snorkeling is more likely to be available at Ke'e Beach unless winter swells are heavy from the north.

But, if you're looking for a place on Kaua'i to escape the rain, get warm (yes, Kaua'i can be cool in the winter), or escape the crowds, Polihale may be your best bet!

GETTING THERE Follow Highway 50 west as far as it goes. When it reaches Kao Road at the Pacific Missile Range Facility (see map, page 145), it becomes dirt road, jogging right, then left at the light. Follow the signs to Polihale State Park as you continue for another five miles. When you come to the large monkeypod tree at the base of the dunes (about three miles from the highway), turn right and follow the dunes to Polihale, which is located at the very end of the road. Do watch the signs carefully because dirt roads lead off in several directions.

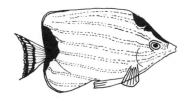

bluestripe butterflyfish

Dive Boats

PADI and NAUI attempt to regulate the diving industry with strict rules, since there are serious risks involved. No one is allowed to dive without certification (a C card). Anyone who wants to dive without proper training is certainly a fool, and the shops who will take such rash people out are equally foolish. We have seen excursions all over the world offering to take people down without proof of certification. This is not the mark of the highest level of safety consciousness. Keep in mind that other advice and services from such operators may be similarly casual. Always take extra care with any rental equipment.

When their business is slow, some take divers (or snorkelers) to sites they can't handle. On the better snorkeling excursions, they keep a close eye on all their charges, so it's like having a lifeguard along.

With a dive boat you may find yourself on the surface as a snorkeler in much rougher conditions than the divers 60 feet beneath you. You'll need to rely on a buddy since the crew is usually more focused on the divers.

Na Pali Coast

The spectacular Na Pali coast begins at Polihale on the west and continues to Ke'e Beach at the other end of the road in the northeast. The unbelievably near-vertical jagged cliffs of this coastline prevent roads of any sort. The only way to see this area up close without a helicopter is either by hiking the eleven-mile long difficult Kalalau Trail, or arriving by water. Excursions are available, including comfortable catamarans, fast and bumpy Zodiac rafts, as well as kayaks when the water is calm enough.

Only the smaller craft can land along the coast, because the reef is relatively shallow along the best beaches. Larger boats will be able to pass by for the gorgeous views of the saw-toothed peaks and tall waterfalls. When seas are somewhat calm, rafts and kayaks can enter the caves, duck under waterfalls, and land on the small, empty beaches, where Kaua'i has two parks.

To see any of this coast by boat, you will need a guide of some sort since conditions can be treacherous at times. However, snorkeling can be surprisingly easy at the protected beaches.

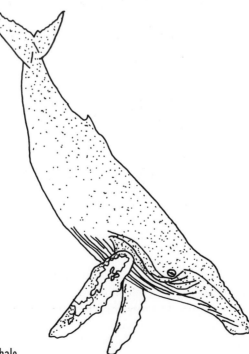

humpback whale

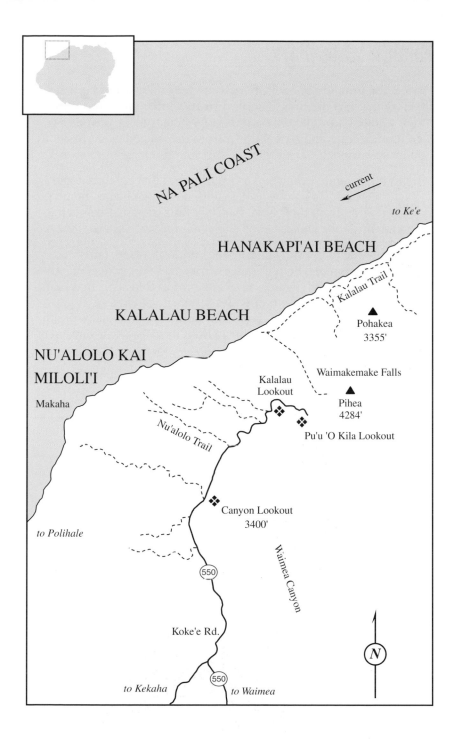

NA PALI COAST

current

to Ke'e

HANAKAPI'AI BEACH

Kalalau Trail

KALALAU BEACH

▲ Pohakea
3355'

NU'ALOLO KAI

Waimakemake Falls

MILOLI'I

Kalalau
Lookout

Makaha

▲ Pihea
4284'

Nu'alolo Trail

Pu'u 'O Kila Lookout

to Polihale

Canyon Lookout
3400'

Waimea Canyon

(550)

Koke'e Rd.

(550)

to Kekaha   to Waimea

N

Miloli'i State Park

Proceeding around the Na Pali coast for four miles from Polihale Park, we come to the first of several worthwhile snorkeling sites: Miloli'i State Park. The only access is by boat, unless you're a mountain climber and rappel down from the rugged peaks at about 5,000-foot altitude.

Miloli'i has a sandy beach and a fringing reef that extends about 250 feet seaward. It's a popular destination for excursions. Some provide snorkeling from their boat, but only rafts are small enough to drop you off on the shore.

Often calm due to the surrounding reef, Miloli'i offers fairly easy entry from the sand. The reef ranges from 2-15 feet under water, so you'll need very calm conditions to be comfortable. This makes for better snorkeling than swimming. It's a fun site to explore, if you stay well away from any big swells. It's unlikely that boats will drop you off here if they have any doubts about its safety. Currents are not a problem here on a calm day.

GETTING THERE   At the far southwest of the Na Pali Coast, this beach is too isolated to access in any way but boat.

Nu'alolo Kai State Park

Similar to Miloli'i and located to the north, this area offers better snorkeling than swimming and is one of the boat destinations. Nu'alolo Kai and Miloli'i both used to be fishing villages, and both contain interesting ruins. Although you can't see them from the beach, Nu'alolo Kai has terraced fields in the valley above.

The fringing reef at Nu'alolo Kai extends out about 500 feet and has a small boat channel in the center wide enough to accommodate kayaks or Zodiac rafts. The wide reef here offers some protection from waves most of the year, but that isn't enough in the heavy winter storms. When calm, the reef area is flat with little current. Entry from shore is easy if you don't mind pebbles and rocks.

When seas are very calm, this entire Na Pali coast offers superb kayaking. When a bit rougher, it offers quite a challenge. This whole coast provides some spectacular viewing either from a distance or up close. Try to do both because the cliffs, caves, beaches and rocky cliffs can best be seen and explored from up close, while the lush

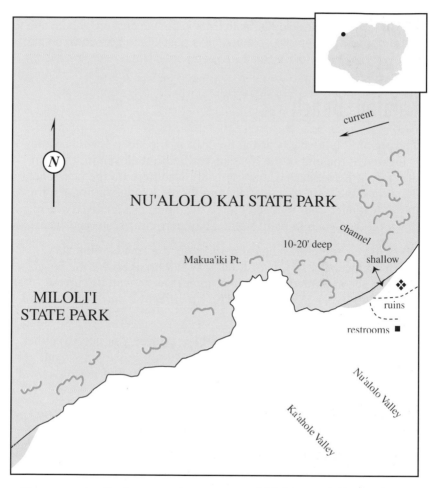

valleys, saw-toothed mountain ranges, and high waterfalls can best be viewed from a bit further out to sea.

These Na Pali beaches, lovely as they may be, attract insects and mice, who make their own living eating what tourists leave behind. When winter swells arrive, snorkeling isn't the best because towering waves crash against these cliffs.

However, as a setting for a calm snorkel in good weather, what could be better? If you don't see too much underwater, you can glance up at the dramatic green mountains in the background. A thoroughly enjoyable way to spend the day! Amenities include restrooms set back from the rocky beach, a couple of covered picnic tables and a short hike to the ruins and heiau. Take care to avoid stepping in the smelly jackfruit that fall onto the trail and rot (picturesquely, of course).

GETTING THERE Nu'alolo Kai State Park is best accessed by boat due to the surrounding steep cliffs, although it is possible to hike down on the Nu'alolo Trail from Koke'e Road – experts only. Not a realistic option.

Kalalau Beach

This incredibly lovely beach at the foot of the steep Kalalau Valley is located at the end of the Kalalau Trail, about eleven miles from the start at Ke'e Beach. Camping is allowed here on the beach near the dunes, but with permits only and there's a long waiting list for these. A ranger does indeed enforce the rules, especially if you're down on the beach in plain sight. They may confiscate your gear!

While it can sometimes be calm and safe, the surf is often very rough on the western side of Kaua'i. When breakers hit the beach, they are accompanied by plenty of undertow as well as currents that can and do sweep people away. The rip current is most often found in the center of the beach.

Other than the eleven-mile difficult hike (where you need to either bring drinking water or treat it), access is only possible by boat. Kayakers sometimes come ashore here when weather permits, but it isn't a snorkeling destination for the excursions.

GETTING THERE Kalalau Beach is an oasis located at the end of the spectacular Kalalau Trail after a difficult eleven-mile hike from Ke'e Beach in northern Kaua'i (see map, page 151). This is not a hike for day-trippers. You can camp with permit only, but these fill a year or more ahead. You'll need to bring or treat any fresh water along the coast. Permits are strictly enforced by an ever-present ranger.

Hanakapi'ai Beach

For those who don't want to hike eleven challenging miles, the Hanakapi'ai Beach is only two miles from the start of Kalalau Trail at Ke'e Beach. This is a steep, and usually slippery, two miles, so most people arrive at the beach wanting to hop in the water. Think again and check out the waves, then opt to splash around in the shallow water protected by a sand bar. Hikers with any energy left can take the tough two-mile hike up to the waterfall.

More folks have drowned at this beach than any other in Kaua'i. Tourists (usually young men) get in trouble here frequently. Once you have been pulled out away from shore, it can be difficult or impossible to return and there's no handy phone for calling the coast guard, or even anyone to help you.

Needless to say, we don't recommend snorkeling here. We do recommend the dramatic and downright breathtaking trail up and down the edge of the Na Pali coast, but try to hike when it hasn't been raining too heavily. Slippery mud does nothing to ease the trip.

GETTING THERE If you want a taste of the dramatic and gorgeous Kalalau Trail, Hanakapi'ai Beach is just two miles from Ke'e Beach in northwestern Kaua'i (see map, page 151). This is a rugged, but spectacular trail to a lovely beach, where you definitely should not swim or snorkel due to the danger of waves and currents. Excursions often follow the Na Pali coast to show you the view, but are unlikely to stop here because there are plenty of safer spots along the Na Pali coast.

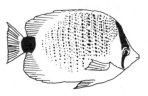

milletseed butterflyfish

Ni'ihau Island

Less than a mile from the northern coast of Ni'ihau, you'll find some top-notch snorkeling at Lehua Island. For those who have been to Molokini (near Maui), Lehua is a similar, bare crescent-shaped rim of a volcanic island. The best snorkeling is usually on the back at the southwestern corner making the snorkeling quite different from the inside of Molokini. And no crowds!

Lehua Island is accessible by boat only and offers some of the clearest water in Hawai'i – a must-try destination for dedicated snorkelers. The back of the island is protected from big northern swells and is close enough to Ni'ihau to gain protection from southern swell. The exact site must be chosen by the captain, but you're likely to find a spot that offers a shallow reef with steep drop-off into the big blue sea.

To give you a brief example of what awaits at Lehua, in one day we saw schools of milletseed butterflyfish, all sorts of butterflyfish including raccoon, fourspot, pyramid, longnose and the saddleback you see on the cover of this book. Wrasses and tangs were abundant as were the pennant butterflyfish seldom seen on other islands. Monk seals rested on the island, dolphins cavorted nearby, and brown-footed boobies flew overhead. If lucky, you may also see whales and/or huge schools of spinner dolphins on the trip.

Water here is crystal clear, so the deep blues of the open ocean set off the bright colors of the reef fish. The reef itself is still in excellent condition. Granted this is a long trip by boat, especially when the sea is high, and it's more expensive than most excursions. Still, you'll be talking about Lehua Island and the trip along the famous Na Pali coastline for years to come.

Even though we didn't go on a particularly calm day, it's a trip we could've happily taken again the very next day. A fast, smooth, very seaworthy boat is preferable because the channel between Kaua'i and Ni'ihau is about twenty miles wide. Although all beaches in Hawai'i are legally available for public use, the island of Ni'ihau has managed to prevent access while trying to retain the traditional isolation for its Hawai'ian-speaking people.

GETTING THERE   While access to Ni'ihau itself is forbidden, boats can lie offshore and snorkel. This is a twenty-mile trip from Port Allen, but it's a beautiful twenty miles and we highly recommend the trip on the speedy catamaran run by Holoholo Charters from Port Allen.

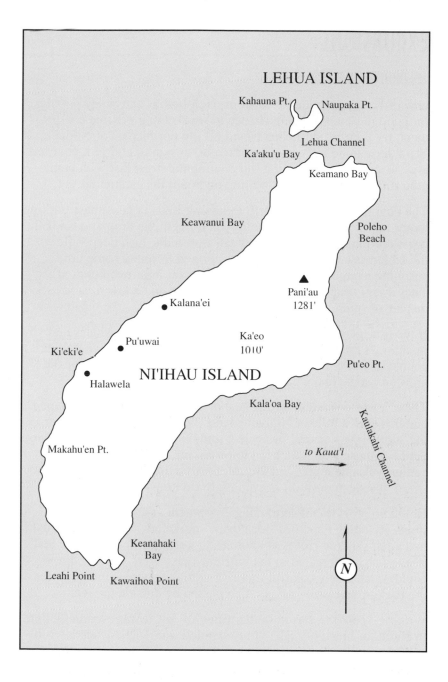

LEHUA ISLAND

Kahauna Pt.   Naupaka Pt.

Lehua Channel

Ka'aku'u Bay

Keamano Bay

Keawanui Bay

Poleho
Beach

▲
Pani'au
1281'

Kalana'ei

Ka'eo
1010'

Ki'eki'e   Pu'uwai

NI'IHAU ISLAND

Pu'eo Pt.

Halawela

Kala'oa Bay

Makahu'en Pt.

to Kaua'i

Kaulakahi Channel

Keanahaki
Bay

Leahi Point   Kawaihoa Point

N

EXCURSIONS

HOLOHOLO CHARTERS

One of Kaua'i's premier excursions, Holoholo is extremely popular for good reason. For a rare chance to snorkel in a pristine environment, try their trip to Lehua Island off the north coast of Ni'ihau. You'll have to be in Port Allen at 6 a.m. to sign in and join your fellow sleepy passengers, but a full continental breakfast with cinnamon rolls and fruit will be waiting on board the catamaran.

The boat heads west and north following Kaua'i's coast past Barking Sands and Polihale. At that point you'll begin the dramatic Na Pali coast portion of the trip. We saw tall waterfalls, lush deep valleys, the fabled saw-toothed ridges, and stopped to spend some time watching a large pod of spinner dolphins (at least two hundred). They swam near the boat, slapped their fins and a few treated us to a display of spinning jumps.

If the time of year is right, there's a chance of seeing whales and manta rays on the trip. Holoholo even stopped to see a whale shark a couple of weeks before our trip. Now that one was a thrill for the crew and some lucky passengers!

Then, it was onward to Lehua Island, a small bare crescent-shaped crater within a mile of Ni'ihau Island. Water here is crystal-clear, the snorkeling site well-protected, and both coral and fish are abundant For those who have been to Molokini, off Maui, Lehua is a similar volcanic crater, but the calm snorkeling here is on the back, where the steep drop-off is even more exciting.

Holoholo provides all snorkeling equipment and various type of floats including "noodles" for novice snorkelers. The area we tried had a flat shallow reef near shore with a steep drop-off (30-70 feet) where fish congregated in the nutrient-rich waters. At the edge we could watch lovely colorful reef fish with the deepest indigo water in the background while pelagic fish passed by outside the reef.

While we could've stayed in the water all day, it was eventually time to board for lunch of make-your-own deli sandwiches, salads, fruit and a variety of drinks (including beer, now that the snorkeling was finished).

Along the back of Lehua, we proceeded to Keyhole Rock (a popular photo op), had a good view of Ni'ihau from the boat, then back across the channel – ending the trip with always-available drinks and lots of chocolate chip macadamia nut cookies.

This is open ocean between the islands, so do take your seasickness remedy if needed. See our recommendation on page 161 because you don't want a silly thing like seasickness to spoil this magical day.

We were surprised to learn that Holoholo doesn't have to cancel often. South swells had been somewhat high before we went, but the trip was quite smooth in this fast and comfortable catamaran. When out in the open channel, do take their words of caution and make use of the many guard-rails to hold on at all times when you're not in a seat.

Holoholo Charters   800-848-6130
www.holoholocharters.com   808-335-0815

KAUA'I SEA TOURS

Kaua'i Sea Tours offers several options for excursions along the Na Pali coast. We tried both the zodiac-type raft with eight passengers and Lucky Lady, a catamaran holding about fifty people.

Take the raft for maximum adventure. It's guaranteed to be bumpy, wet, thrilling, with full exposure to the sun. They don't take anyone who is pregnant or has serious back or neck trouble – for obvious reasons. If you want an easy trip, choose the bigger boat, but for a ton of fun, nothing beats the raft if you're rough and tough enough.

The rafting trip begins with coffee and sweet rolls in the office. Don't forget to use the restroom, as it is several hours before any stop. There are no restrooms on board, so you need to ask for a stop and hop in the water to relieve yourself. We set out from Port Allen with stops along the way to see dolphins and turtles. At the start of the Na Pali coast we zipped from valley to cave to cliff. At times the raft entered smallish caves, drove under a waterfall, and explored many of the nooks and crannies along this gorgeous coastline.

One of more interesting stops was in a cave where the entire top opened up to the sky. The cliffs along the side of the cave were about sixty feet straight up. While the rafts can explore this coastline all year, they can only enter the caves when north swells aren't too high, and are less likely to encounter such good conditions during winter storms.

The narration was fascinating, though a little hard to hear when the raft was on the move – especially from the back of the raft. Eventually we returned to Nu'alolo Kai Beach. The raft edged right in close to shore, where we enjoyed the picnic lunches at the tables set in a covered shelter. Quite a picturesque picnicking spot!

Snorkeling was in a calm area right in front with relatively easy entry from the shore. The reef here is 5-15' deep with plenty of space to wander. This isn't a spectacular site with big numbers of fish, but we had excellent views of some very colorful ones. If you look very close, you might also see octopuses here.

For a more sedate trip, try the Lucky Lady, a comfortable boat with a nice set-up for snorkelers to enter the water. They too provide all equipment as well as breakfast and lunch onboard. They slice through the swells in the channel, but still provided enough bounce in the front of the boat, where they allowed some brave passengers to sit on the "trampoline" and bounce their way back to port – entertaining the whole group.

For snorkeling, the Lucky Lady took us to Miloli'i along the cliffs of the Na Pali coast. If you are an experienced snorkeler and have a chance, sign up to go one cove further on their raft (which makes a rendezvous here with Lucky Lady) because the snorkeling is a bit better at Nu'alolo Kai Beach. That's also an interesting way to have a comfortable ride up, and a touch of rafting adventure, too.

Beginners will probably want to stay with the Lucky Lady The staff is alert to provide whatever it takes to make you comfortable in the water and out. For first-time snorkelers, you won't find a boat with a better arrangement for entry and exit.

Depending on the season, Sea Tours offers 4, 5, or 6-hour snorkeling trips as well as sunset excursions and whale watching.

Kaua'i Sea Tours   800-733-7997
www.kauaiseatours.com   808-826-7254

SEA FUN KAUA'I

While this company offers a variety of trips around Kaua'i, we've sampled just their snorkeling trip. This half-day shore-based trip will vary the location depending on current ocean conditions. They pick you at at most hotels, and provide all gear, snacks and lunch.

Each tour is led by an expert with knowledge of the area to be snorkeled. They welcome non-swimmers and have plenty of aids such as float boards if needed. The whole group snorkels together with more advanced snorkelers allowed to explore nearby. Our snorkel van headed to Tunnels on a fairly calm day, spending a full two hours in the water as the group slowly drifted along the reef. After our snorkel, the van met us at the edge of the sand and gave us all a ride down to Ha'ena State Park for showers and lunch.

Motion Sickness

Motion sickness (seasickness or carsickness) is a minor inner ear disorder which can really cut into your pleasure on the water, on long, curvy road trips or in choppy air. Fortunately, motion sickness is quite controllable these days. All it takes is a little advance planning to turn a potentially miserable experience into a normal, fun one. Don't let old fears keep you from great water adventures anymore.

Mel can get seasick just by vividly imagining a rocking boat, so he has tried just about every remedy personally. These field trials are a messy business, so we'll spare you the details, and just pass on what really works in our experience.

Forget the wrist pressure-point bands – they don't do the job for anyone we've ever met. You might as well put them in the closet along with your ultrasonic pest repeller, in our opinion.

The most effective remedy we've found so far is Meclizine, a pill available by prescription only. It works perfectly for Mel with no noticeable side effects. Alcohol can interact with it to make you drowsy. We learned about Meclizine when Jon Carroll, a columnist in the San Francisco Chronicle, reported that it had sufficed for him in 15-25' swells on the way to Antarctica. If it does the job there, it should handle all but the most radical of snorkeling excursions.

An over-the-counter alternative is Benadryl usually used as a decongestant. It can also be effective against motion sickness. Ginger is also used but may not be strong enough for some people.

Use these medicines carefully and only after consulting your doctor. In some cases, you must avoid alcohol, other drugs or diving, since these medications can produce drowsiness.

This is a good way for beginners (especially children) to learn to snorkel and head out to deeper water with supervision. The leader of our group was extremely patient and made sure that everyone was comfortable. Worth checking out, especially if being in a group makes you more comfortable in the water.

Sea Fun Kaua'i   808-245-6400

LAND EXCURSIONS

KOKE'E STATE PARK

Koke'e State Park should not be missed. The Waimea Canyon on the way is lovely, and the view of the Kalalau Valley is absolutely spectacular. If you happen to arrive in the clouds, which is not unusual here where it rains 500 inches in a year, just wait for half an hour. It can clear in a matter of minutes as clouds sweep on by. If it isn't raining too hard, stay to enjoy the many trails stretching out from the overlook. Bring at least a sweater because it's much cooler up here even when the sun is out. If you're heading off for a hike, be prepared for rain and mud.

Forty-five miles of trails branch out in all directions, so pick up a map at the ranger's station at the Koke'e Museum. Then head out to the Alakai Swamp, the Sugi Grove area, down to the floor of the Waimea Canyon, or just walk to the lookout points. Looking out over the vast Kalalau Valley, with the faint bleating of wild goats echoing off the lush green valley walls, is special and memorable.

KALALAU TRAIL

To see the Kalalau Valley from the beach, all you need to do is hike eleven miles over rugged terrain from the start of the trail at Ke'e Beach in the far northwest. Permits are required and enforced, so this must be planned about a year ahead of time. All water has to be brought in or treated.

To get a taste of this gorgeous trail, hike the two miles in to Hanakapi'ai Beach. This is a beautiful big beach, but far too dangerous for water sports. The water is awfully tempting though, so Hanakapi'ai Beach has the record number of deaths by drowning for all of Kaua'i.

KAYAKING

Kaua'i has a number of rivers available for easy kayaking, from the Hanalei River in the north, the Kalihiwai River in the north, the Kapa'a River in the east, to the Waimea River in the south.

When the ocean is calm enough, there are wonderful opportunities to kayak the Na Pali coast. Here, you're likely to need a guide for safety and to find the hidden treasures. In the south, kayaking is especially good in the Kipu Kai area, available only by permission.

BIKING

Kaua'i offers excellent opportunities to explore the island by bike. Kapa'a has a bike trail along the coast off the main highway. The northwest from Hanalei to Ha'ena is picturesque although the road is narrow. The Hanalei Valley is perfect for biking along the river. Po'ipu offers smaller roads along the coast to the west. For rugged bikers, the Powerline Trail leads from Princeville twelve miles up across the Anahola Mountains.

All sorts of bike tours are available including some that advertise as "downhill only." See current offerings in the many free activities guides.

MOVIE LOCATIONS

Over the years, Kaua'i has attracted movie makers looking for gorgeous tropical scenery. First was "South Pacific", which brought fame to Lumahai Beach as the imaginary tropical paradise Bali Hai. Other movies include "Jurassic Park" with its jungle scenery filmed in northeast Kaua'i, "Thornbirds" with scattered locations in the west and northwest. "6 Days and 7 Nights" shot in multiple locations, and "Blue Hawaii" with Elvis Presley, shot in Kapa'a and Po'ipu. There are special movie theme sightseeing excursions, if you're a real fan.

AIR EXCURSIONS

Kaua'i is one of world's most spectacular spots for helicopter sightseeing. This is an expensive, but memorable trip – with a variety of flight plans, all passing over the spectacular Na Pali coast. Kaua'i is possibly even more beautiful from the air. Helicopters give you a chance to see the incredible saw-toothed ridges with their tall waterfalls. Since Mount Wai'ale'ale receives about 500 inches of rain each year, plenty of waterfalls drop off its steep sides. Add the multitude of rainbows and isolated beaches for scenery that can't be beat.

From the south, flights leave from the Lihu'e helicopter airport located across 'Ahukini Road from the main terminal (see maps, page 111 and 113).

From the north, flights leave from the small Princeville Airport, located on the mountain side of Highway 56 east of Princeville (see map, page 79).

From the west, fly from Hanapepe (see map, page 139).

Marine Life

The coral reef supports tremendous diversity in a small space. On a healthy reef, you've never seen everything, because of the boggling variety of species, as well as changes from day to day and changes from day to night. The reef functions much like the oasis in the desert providing food (more abundant than the open ocean) and shelter from predators. Only the wild rain forests can compare with the reef in complexity.

In Hawai'i the reef coral itself is less spectacular than in warmer waters of the world. This is counterbalanced by the colorful and abundant fish, which provide quite a show.

There are excellent color fish identification cards available in bookstores and dive shops. We particularly like the ones published by Natural World Press. There are also many good marine life books that give far more detailed descriptions of each creature than we attempt in these brief notes.

OCTOPUS

Some varieties of octopuses hide during the day; others will hunt for food then. They eat shrimp, fish, crabs, and mollusks – you should eat so well! Octopuses have strong "beaks" and can bite humans, so it's safer to not handle them.

Being mollusks without shells, they must rely on speed, cunning and camouflage to escape danger. Octopuses are capable of imitating a flashing sign, or changing their color and texture to match their surroundings in an instant. This makes them very hard to spot, even when they're hiding in plain sight – usually on the bottom or on rocks. They also squirt an ink to confuse predators or prey. They live about two years.

Just because you haven't seen one does not mean they aren't there. Go slow and watch carefully for the "rock" that moves.

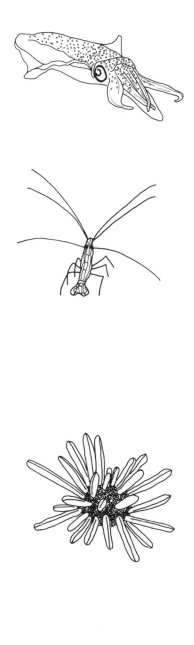

REEF SQUID

These graceful, iridescent creatures hang around reef areas, often forming a single long line. All eyes will follow you easily since they have 360 degree vision. They can capture surprisingly large fish with their tentacles.

SHRIMP

In all kinds, colors, and sizes, they like to hide in rocks and coral – often living symbiotically with the coral. They are difficult to spot during the daytime, but at night you will notice lots of tiny pairs of eyes reflected in the flashlight beam. Most are fairly small and well-disguised.

Some examples include: the harlequin shrimp (brightly colored) that eat sea stars, the banded coral shrimp (found all over the world), and numerous tiny shrimp that you won't see without magnification.

SEA URCHINS

Concealed tube feet allow urchins to move around in their hunt for algae. The collector urchin has pebbles and bits of coral attached for camouflage. These urchins are quite common in Hawai'i, and have no spines.

Beware of purple-black urchins with long spines. These are common in shallow water at certain beaches. It's not the long spines that get you, it's the ones beneath. The bright red pencil sea urchin is common and easy to spot. Although large, its spines aren't sharp enough to be a problem for people.

CRINOIDS

These animals seen on top of the rocks or coral can easily be mistaken for plants. They are sometimes called "feather stars" and are delicate and beautiful plankton feeders.

SEA STARS

Abundant, in many colors and styles. The crown of thorns sea star, which can be such a devastator of coral reefs, is found in Hawai'i, but not in large numbers like the South Pacific. Sea stars firmly grasp their prey with strong suction cups, and then eat at leisure.

RAYS

Manta rays (large plankton-eaters) use two flaps to guide plankton into their huge efficient mouths. Mantas often grow to be two meters from wing-tip to wing-tip, and can weigh 300 pounds. They can't sting, but are large enough to bump hard.

Mantas feed at night by doing forward rolls in the water with mouths wide open. Lights will attract plankton which appeal to the manta rays. Dive boats in favored locations can easily attract them with their bright lights making the night trips quite exciting.

Another beautiful ray, the spotted eagle ray, can sometimes be seen cruising the bottom for food and can grow to be seven feet across. They have a dark back with lots of small white dots and an extremely long tail. Their fins function more like wings to enable them to "fly" along rather than swimming.

Common sting rays prefer the sandy bottom and stay in calm, shallow, warmer water.

EELS

Many types of moray eels abound among the reefs of Kaua'i. They can easily grow up to two meters long.

Varieties of moray found in Hawai'i include whitemouth, snowflake, zebra (black and white stripes), wavy-lined, mottled, and dragon moray (often reddish-brown with distinct white spots of differing sizes).

Morays prefer to hide in holes during the day. If out cruising, they often find a nearby hole when spotting a snorkeler. When they stick out their heads and breathe, their teeth are most impressive.

Eels generally have no interest in eating snorkelers, other than very annoying ones, while they are quite happy and able to swallow a fairly large fish.

TRUMPETFISH

These long, skinny fish can change color, often bright yellow or light green – and will change right in front of your eyes. They sometimes hang upright to blend with their environment, lying in wait to suck in their prey. Sometimes they shadow another fish to sneak up on prey – even at a cleaning station.

They do eat during the day, which is unusual for fish-eaters, who usually eat at dawn or dusk. Trumpetfish are quite common in Kaua'i and often seen alone. Some grow to more than one meter long.

NEEDLEFISH

These pointed, common silvery-blue fish like swimming very near the surface, usually in schools – occasionally leaping from the water. All types of needlefish are long and skinny as their name implies, and grow to as much as 1-2 feet long. Color and markings vary, but the long narrow shape is distinctive and hard to mistake. They're usually bluish on top, and translucent below for camouflage.

BUTTERFLYFISH

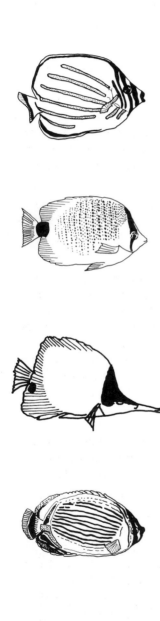

Butterflyfish are beautiful, colorful, abundant and varied in Hawai'i. They have incredible coloration, typically bright yellow, white, orange, black, and sometimes a little blue. They hang out near coral, eating algae, sponges, tube worms and coral polyps. No one really understands the purpose of their beautiful colors, but many have speculated. Perhaps they serve territorial needs.

Juveniles are often distinctly different in coloring. Bizarre patterns may confuse predators – especially since they can pivot fast. Bars may help some hide, while stripes are seen more in faster fish. Black lines across the eyes and spots near the tail also confuse predators.

Butterflyfish are often seen in pairs remaining together for up to three years. They're delightful to watch. Hovering and turning are more important to them than speed since they stay near shelter of the reef and catch a quick meal – like a tube worm.

The ones you are most likely to see in Hawai'i include: raccoon (reminding you of the face of the animal), ornate (with bright orange lines making it easy to spot), threadfin (another large, beautiful one), saddleback, lemon (very tiny), bluestripe (a beautiful one found only in Hawai'i), fourspot, milletseed, oval, teardrop, and forceps (also called long nose). The lined butterflyfish is the largest variety found in Hawai'i.

Many butterflyfish have black spots near the tail – perhaps to confuse a predator about which way they're headed. Watch and they may confuse you too.

PARROTFISH

Among the most dramatically colored fish on the reef, male parrotfish are blue, green, turquoise, yellow, lavender, and/or orange with endless variations of these colors. Females tend to be reddish brown. No two are alike. Parrotfish are very beautiful, with artistic, abstract markings.

These fish change colors at different times in their lives and can also change sex as needed. They can be quite large (up to one meter).

Patient grazers, they spend countless hours scraping algae from dead coral with their large, beak-like teeth, and create tons of white sand in the process. Most prefer to zoom away from snorkelers, but you'll see them passing gracefully by and will hear them crunching away at the coral.

TRIGGERFISH

Fond of sea urchins as a main course, triggerfish graze during the day on algae, worms and other small items.

Varieties include the Picasso (wildly colorful – not too many at each beach, but worth watching for), reef (the Hawai'ian state fish), pinktail (easy to identify with its black body, white fins and pink tail), black (common, distinctive white lines between body and fins). The checkerboard triggerfish has a pink tail, yellow-edged fins, and blue stripes on its face. All triggerfish are very beautiful and fascinating to watch.

FILEFISH

The scrawled filefish has blue scribbles and brown dots over its olive green body. Quite large, up to one meter, often in pairs, but seen occasionally in groups.

A filefish will often turn its body flat to your view, and raise its top spine in order to impress you. This lets you have a great close-up view – a perfect photo opportunity.

The brown filefish (endemic) is much smaller, with lines on its head and white spots on its brown body. The fantail filefish (also endemic and small) has a distinct orange tail and lots of black spots over a light body. Filefish will sometimes change color patterns rapidly for camouflage.

SURGEONFISH

Razor-sharp fin-like spines on each side of the tail are the hallmark of this fish, quite common in Hawai'i. These spines provide excellent defense, but aren't needed to fend off tourists since surgeonfish can easily swim away.

Varieties includes the orangeband surgeonfish (with distinctive long, bright orange marks on the side), as well as the Achilles tang (also called naso tang), which has bright orange spots surrounding the spines near the orange tail. The yellow tang is completely yellow and smaller. The sailfin tang has dramatic vertical markings. It's less common, but easy to identify.

WRASSES

Wrasses are amazingly bright and multicolored fish. Some very small ones set themselves up for business and operate a cleaning station, where they clean much larger fish without having to worry about becoming dinner. They eat parasites, and provide an improbable reef service in the process. Perhaps their bright colors serve as neon signs to advertise their services Hang out near their cleaning stations for excellent fish viewing. In Hawai'i, the cleaner wrasse is bright yellow, purple and black.

Other wrasses are large including the dazzling yellowtail (up to 15 inches), which has a red body covered with glowing blue spots, a few stripes, and a bright yellow tail.

Another large wrasse, the saddleback, is endemic to Hawai'i. It is bright blue, with green and orange markings. Wrasses are closely related to parrotfish. Like parrotfish, they can change colors and sex.

SCORPIONFISH

This improbable-looking fish is very colorful, with feather-like multicolor spines. Beware of their poisonous spines, though! Don't even think about touching a scorpionfish, and try to avoid accidentally stepping on one.

This varied group of exotic fish includes the bright red Hawai'ian turkeyfish, sometimes called a lionfish.

Others are so well-camouflaged that they are hard to see. They just lurk on the bottom blending in well with the sand and coral. If you see one, count yourself lucky.

PUFFERFISH

Pufferfish (and the related trunkfish) swim slowly, so need more protection. Some can blow up like balloons when threatened.

Two kinds are common in sheltered areas: porcupine (displaying spines when inflated), and spotted trunkfish and boxfish (often brown or black with lots of white dots). They tend to prefer to escape under the coral, although some seem unafraid of snorkelers.

SHARKS

Although sharks have quite a reputation for teeth rather than brains, they are unquestionably survivors, having been around for about 300 million years.

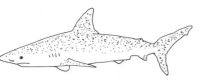

This is an extremely successful species with keen hearing, smell, sight and ability to detect electrical signals through the water. They swim with a side-to-side motion, which does not make them speedy by ocean standards.

When snorkeling you are unlikely to spot any shark except the reef or white-tipped lazing around shallow water. Plenty of larger species pass by Hawai'i, but tend to prefer the deeper waters in the channels.

DOLPHINS

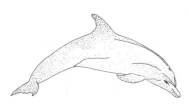

Spinner dolphins are frequently seen in large schools (about 200). They swim as small family groups within these schools, and often swim fast, leaping from the water, spinning in the air. They tend to hang out in certain locations, so you can search them out if you like.

Bottlenose dolphins often approach fast-moving boats, and it is a great thrill to watch them race along just next to the bow of your boat, jumping in and out of the water with grace and easy speed.

Beaked and spotted dolphins are also commonly seen in Hawai'i.

SEA TURTLES

Common at many Kaua'i reefs, though they usually stay away from humans. Some do seem nearly tame – or at least unconcerned about snorkelers.

Sea turtles are often seen in pairs. Larger specimens (often seen at The Cliffs or Ho'ai Bay) might be more than 100 years old, and tend to be docile and unafraid. You'll often see them resting on the bottom in about ten to twenty feet of water during the day. They will let you swim as close as you like, but if you hover over them, they might be afraid to come up for air. Just before dusk, they often hunt for food along the coast.

Do not disturb these graceful creatures, so that they can remain unafraid to swim among snorkelers. In Hawai'i it is against the law to touch or harass these magnificent animals.

WHALES

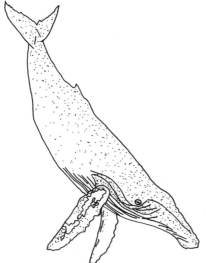

Humpback whales migrate here to breed in winter, around early-December. Humpbacks come quite close to the coast, where you can watch whole families. They are so large that you can often easily see them spouting and breaching. If you bring binoculars, you can see them well from shore. Their great size never fails to impress, as does their fluid, seemingly effortless graceful movement in the water.

Weather

All islands have a windward side, which is wetter, and a leeward side which is drier. In Hawai'i, the northeast is windward and hence wet, and the southwest is leeward, or kona, and hence drier and sunnier. Waves from afar tend to arrive from the north in winter and from the south in summer, although this pattern changes often.

Hawai'i gets most of its rain in the winter. The most severe storms (called kona), however, come from the south and can even bring hurricanes in the summer. Temperatures tend to be very mild year-round, yet there is variety around Kaua'i on any day of the year. There are days when you could tan in Po'ipu in the morning, drive up to cool Koke'e Park later, while rain continues in Hanalei. Summer temperatures are five degrees F warmer than winter.

Evaporating moisture from the ocean forms clouds. As the clouds rise over the mountains, they cool, and the condensing moisture becomes rain. Mount Wai'ale'ale receives 500 inches of rain a year, while Po'ipu only gets about 20 inches.

Having lost most of their moisture in passing over the mountains, the clouds have little left for the leeward side – so it is in the rain shadow of the mountains. The leeward weather is therefore often sunny. Waikiki, Poipu, Ka'anapali, and Kona are all in rain shadows. On Kaua'i, if you get stuck with heavy rains in Hanalei, just head for Po'ipu to find the sun.

Changeable is the word for Kaua'i's weather – not just between areas, but also rapidly changeable in any given place. The trade winds blow about 90% of the time in the summer and about 50% in the winter. They tend to be stronger in the afternoon and are stronger on Kaua'i than the other Hawai'ian islands.

The windward or northeastern coasts have much more rain, wind and waves – something important to remember when snorkeling.

Christmas wrasse

Seasonal Changes

Kaua'i has much milder weather than the continental United States, yet it is has seasons you might call winter, spring and summer. At 20°N Latitude, there are nearly 2 1/2 hours more sun in midsummer than in midwinter, which is 21% more. But the moderating effect of the ocean keeps temperature swings quite moderate.

Winter is the cooler, wetter season. Cooler is a relative term, as the average high temperature in winter falls to a brisk 80° F, as opposed to a summer average high of 88° F. Water temperature in winter falls to around 77° F, and at times, wind, rain and cooler air temperatures can temper your desire to splash around in the water. Winter usually begins in mid-November, with the start of winter storms from the north-northwest. This is the start of the large wave season on the north coast. Winter tails off in mid-March.

Spring really is just the transition from winter to summer, and is marked by the end of winter storms in mid-March. Hours of sunshine go up, especially on the west, leeward side of the island. This can be a very pleasant time of year. Spring transitions into summer in May.

Summer begins in May, as the weather warms, and the rains slacken. Trade winds temper the heat and humidity almost all the time. This is prime sunning and play time. An occasional tropical storm or hurricane can come through, and swells can roll in from the south. The heat softens in October as summer draws to an end.

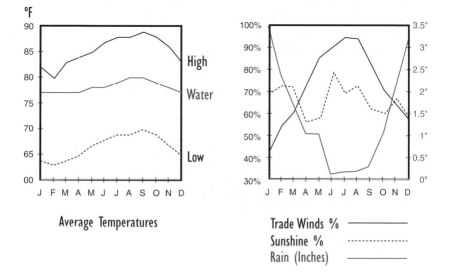

Average Temperatures

Trade Winds % ————————
Sunshine %   ------------------
Rain (Inches) ————————

Month by Month

JANUARY: This month offers an opportunity for the wettest weather all year. It's also one of the coolest. Large surf can often pound the north and west exposed beaches.

FEBRUARY: Just as cool, the surf continues to hit the north and west exposed beaches, although storms are a bit less frequent.

MARCH: The weather starts to improve with fewer storms, especially in the west.

APRIL: Spring arrives early, so warm weather begins during this month.

MAY: Summer is already arriving – especially in the south and west. This tends to be a trouble-free month.

JUNE: This offers very warm and dry weather with plenty of sun. Fortunately the winds blow nearly every day.

JULY: Much the same as June, except that storms in the South Pacific begin at this time. They hit beaches exposed to the south.

AUGUST: Another warm month, occasional big waves can hit the southern exposed beaches.

SEPTEMBER: This last month of summer can sometimes be the hottest and most humid. Hurricanes can strike Kaua'i, and are most common this month. Most will miss the islands, but bring muggy weather. Iniki, however, brought widespread damage to Kaua'i.

OCTOBER: Milder weather begins this month with the start of storms arriving from the north.

NOVEMBER: Sometimes the first real winter storms arrive and they can be somewhat cool.

DECEMBER: This is winter with frequent storms and wind bringing big waves to the exposed northern and western beaches. However, even this month can be clear and warm between storms.

Coolest month:	February
Hottest month:	September
Rainiest month:	January
Driest month:	June
Coolest water:	December-April
Warmest water:	August-September

Tides

Tides are very slight in Kaua'i, with the average difference between high and low only 2-3 feet max. It's a good idea to know which way the tide is going because tidal flow does affect the currents. If the tide is going out, you might want to avoid snorkeling in places where water is already shallow or currents tend to sweep out of a bay, often the center, or a gap in the reef (see Understanding waves, page 27). Tides matter more in Kaua'i than the other islands.

Water Temperature

On the surface, the water in Hawai'i averages a low of about 77° F (25° C) in March to a high of about 80° F (27° C) in September. Sheltered bays can be a bit warmer, while deeper or rough water can be surprisingly cool. Kaua'i, being further north, can be even cooler. If you happen to be slender, no longer young, or from a moderate climate, this can seem cooler than you might like – especially if you like to snorkel for hours.

Hurricanes

Summer is hurricane season, but it is also the time when weather is typically excellent. While the storms don't last long, they can be terribly destructive. Hurricanes can bring amazingly heavy rain and winds to all the islands. Any of the islands could receive a direct hit, which happened when Hurricanes Ewa and Iniki clobbered Kaua'i.

Tsunamis

Huge waves can be triggered by earthquakes either in the islands or far across the Pacific. They've hit Hawai'i numerous times, more often from the north. Some very destructive tsunamis have hit and swept over the lowest land. Depending on the exact direction, they can directly hit a valley and really wipe it out and rinse it clean. It is probably better to not be there when this happens, unless you're one great surfer dude. Tsunami waves are often spaced as far as fifteen minutes apart.

Currently there's plenty of warning and authorities prefer to warn of every possible tsunami just to be safe. It doesn't pay to ignore warnings just because the sea appears calm. If a major earthquake strikes while you're visiting, it's a good idea to head rapidly for high ground. Leave bays or valleys which can act to funnel the effects of a large wave.

Geology

To understand what's happening today in Hawai'i, begin by casting your thoughts back about 30 million years. At that time lava was bubbling out in the middle of the Pacific about 20,000' below the ocean surface, due to a volcanic hot spot directly underneath. Molten rock pushing up through the ocean floor formed volcanoes under the sea. Lava built up, layer after layer, until it finally reached the surface to form the first island.

As the volcanoes grew, the weight of these early islands gradually caused them to sink down again, forming atolls. The Pacific Plate drifted northwest, while the hot spot remained stationary. A long string of more than 30 islands were formed, stretching from Midway Island southeast 1600 miles all the way to the Big Island. Another island is already rising in the sea close to the southeast side of the Big Island. Loihi Sea Mount is now just 3000' under the surface, and will probably join the Big Island as it emerges. Lava flowing into the sea from Kilauea has been intermittently building the Big Island daily toward Loihi.

Most of the current above-water mass is now concentrated in eight islands. Kaua'i, about 5 million years old, is the oldest of these, while the Big Island is less than 1 million years old. As these islands drift approximately 4 inches northwest each year, the lava conduits to their volcanoes bend until new conduits are formed. Eventually, the next volcano in the chain takes over the job of releasing the unremitting pressure from pools of magma far below.

And a Little Natural History, Too

When each underground mountain emerges from the sea, coral larvae begin to establish their new homes on the volcanic rocks around the base. Stony coral is one of the first ocean creatures to reach and become established on a new island.

These larvae travel island by island – originally coming in a very round-about fashion on the currents from the ancient reefs surrounding Indonesia. Once they became established, it was easier for new larvae to reach the next nearby island. The reef begins as a fringe around the island. Each polyp of coral secretes a skeleton of calcium carbonate. Gradually the colony grows large enough to provide a home for other plants and animals.

All of the major Hawai'ian islands now have fringing reefs around much of the shore. The Big Island, still in formation, is not yet fully surrounded by reef. As the islands grow, get heavy and gradually sink, the reef changes as well. The older islands of Kaua'i and O'ahu have very old coral reef deposits on land – remnants of a time when the sea level was higher.

Coral reefs are made up of coral animals and algae growing on top of the dead skeletons of former creatures. In search of sunlight, they continue to grow upward toward the light, as they need to stay within 150 feet of the surface of the sea.

The outside of a reef grows faster than the inner surface, so eventually a lagoon forms between the reef and the land. The reef is then called a barrier reef, limited examples of which can be found in Kaua'i and O'ahu.

Since the currents in Hawai'i come mainly from Japan rather than the warmer south Pacific, they bring less variety of sea life. Larvae need to survive long enough to reach an island and establish themselves before sending out the next generation, so it's helpful to have stepping-stone islands in order to have greater variety. Most will not survive long enough to cross the large open Pacific ocean.

Tahiti, for example, has a much greater variety of coral because of the stepping-stone islands leading all the way from Southeast Asia. Hawai'i, in contrast, is one of the most isolated island groups in the world. It also has somewhat cooler water and less sunlight than Tahiti, making it less hospitable to some species. This isolation has kept all species of plant and animal life rather limited, and also encouraged the evolution of unique species found only in Hawai'i. These unique species are referred to as endemic. They give Hawai'i a special character – both above and below the water. More than 30% of the fish seen here are found nowhere else in the world.

For millions of years the Hawai'ian Islands had no plants or animals in spite of the rich soil, due to their 2000 mile isolation from other large land masses. When plants and animals finally did arrive, they found little competition and a superb climate. The lack of competition meant plants did not require thorns or other protective features. Some plants and animals found such a perfect environment that they thrived. Before man arrived, Hawai'i had no fruits or vegetables. The Polynesians, and later arrivals, changed this environment enormously by their imports and cultivation.

Most of the "exotic" plants that you may think of as quintessentially Hawai'ian were brought by man (mango, papaya, pineapple, orchid, ginger, hibiscus). Koa and ohia (the Hawai'ian state tree), on the other hand, pre-date man's arrival. Ohia is often the first to grow on lava flows and has produced much of the Hawai'ian rain forest.

Unfortunately, most of the rain forest has already been destroyed by animals brought by man (such as cattle and goats) or cleared to provide land for sugar production. Sugar and pineapple production now appear to be on the way out, a casualty of world economics. Tourism has now replaced these crops, but takes its own toll on the fragile islands of Hawai'i.

Reef Development

Hawai'ian reefs have weathered at least four major changes in the distant past. Many land-based plants and animals also became extinct during these changes and others took their place. Current reefs are composed mostly of shallow water reef coral. They incorporate algae in their structure, and the algae is dependent on photosynthesis.

Different plants and animals live in the varied locations on the reef depending primarily on wave action. Species living on the outer edge of the reef are skilled at surviving strong waves and currents. Lagoon species don't have to endure this, so the lagoon supports more delicate life.

Hawai'i has a number of strikingly different reef habitats – each with its own story to tell. Where the water is rough, cauliflower coral dominates. The more delicate finger coral grows only in the calm lagoon areas. Large boulders are common in the open waters, especially where wave action is heaviest, and they support entirely different creatures. Caves, caverns and old lava tubes are abundant here. Steep drop-offs (like the back of Lehua Island) serve as an upwelling source of plankton-rich water, which attracts many larger creatures to feed. Sandy habitat is found in abundance on Kaua'i. A thriving reef is developing around much of the island.

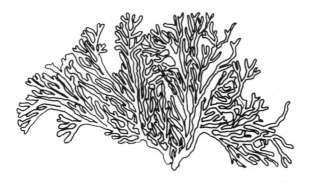

Language

English is now the official language of the islands of Hawai'i – except for the island of Ni'ihau. However, most place names and lots of slang are Hawai'ian, so it's helpful to at least be able to pronounce Hawai'ian enough to be understood. It's a very straight-forward phonetic language – each letter usually pronounced just one way. The long place names aren't nearly so daunting when you've learned the system.

All syllables begin with a consonant that is followed by at least one vowel. When the missionaries attempted to write this spoken language, they used only seven consonants (h,k,l,m,n,p,w) and five vowels (a,e,i,o,u). More recently, in an effort to help outsiders pronounce Hawai'ian, the glottal stop (called an 'okina) has been added – marked by '. For example, in Hawai'i, the ' is used to indicate that each i should be pronounced separately: Ha-wai-i, rather than Ha-waii.

A horizontal line (called a macron) is sometimes placed over vowels to be given a longer duration. Nene, for example, is "Naay-Naay". Unfortunately, our typeface doesn't allow macrons. Each and every letter is pronounced in Hawai'ian, except for a few vowel combinations. However, locals often shorten names a bit, so listen carefully to the way natives pronounce a name. Another addition to the language is a form of pidgin, which served to ease the difficulties of having multiple languages spoken. Laborers were brought in speaking Japanese, Mandarin, Cantonese, Portuguese, English, as well as other languages, and they had to be able to work together. Pidgin evolved as an ad hoc, but surprisingly effective way to communicate, and much of it survives in slang and common usage today.

Pronunciation

Consonants are pronounced the same as in English, except that the W sometimes sounds more like a V when it appears in the middle of a word. Vowels are pronounced as follows:

a = long as in father
e = short as in den, or long as the ay in say
i = long as the ee in sea
o = round as in no
u = round as the ou in you

When vowels are joined (as they often are), pronounce each, with slightly more emphasis on the first one. This varies with local usage.

Commonly Used Vocabulary and Place Names

'a'a = rough lava (of Hawai'ian origin, now used worldwide)

'ahi = tuna, especially yellowfin (albacore) tuna

ahupua'a = land division in pie shape from mountain to sea

ali'i = chief

aloha = hello, goodbye, expressing affection

haole = foreigner (now usually meaning a white person)

heiau = temple, religious platform

hula = native Hawai'ian dance

humuhumunukunukuapua'a = trigger fish that is Hawai'ian state fish

imu = pit for steaming food over hot stones

kahuna = powerful priest

kai = sea

kama'aina = long-time resident of the islands

kane = male

kapu = taboo

ko'ala = barbequed

kokua = help

kona = leeward, or away from the direction of the wind

kukui = candlenut (state tree)

lei = garland of flowers, shells, etc. given as a symbol of affection

lu'au = Hawai'ian traditional feast, including roast pork and poi

mahalo = thanks; admiration, praise, respect

mahimahi = dolphinfish (not a dolphin)

makai = on the seaside, towards the sea, or in that direction

malihini = recent arrival to the islands, tourist, stranger

mana = power coming from the spirit world

mano = shark

mauka = upland, towards the mountains

mauna = mountain, peak

menehune = little people of legend, here before the Polynesians

moana = ocean

nene = Hawai'ian state bird

niu = coconut

ohana = extended family

ono = the best, delicious, savory; to relish or crave

pahoehoe = lava that has a smooth texture (used worldwide)

paka lolo = marijuana

pali = cliff

pupu = appetizer, snack

taro (Polynesian word) = starchy rootplant used to make poi

wahine = female

wai = fresh water

wana = sea urchin

Often Heard Myths

- **"You'll probably never see a shark."**

  If you snorkel often, you probably will see one occasionally, a reef shark, not a Great White or Tiger Shark. Most sharks aren't interested in you for dinner. If you look at actual statistics, your time is better spent worrying about lightning.

- **"Barracudas are harmless to humans."**

  Perhaps some are quite innocuous, but others have bitten off fingers or hands. The Great Barracuda has been involved in the majority of cases we've read. Don't worry about one that has been hanging out in front of a hotel for years, but you may not want to crowd them either. I'd be even more cautious about eating one for dinner, because they are a definite, major cause of ciguatera "fish poisoning". They are one of the best tasting fish, though, in our experience. Feeling lucky?

- **"Jewelry attracts barracuda bites."**

  I first heard this rumor from a 12-year-old, and it was later reinforced by numerous books. The idea is that the flash will fool a barracuda into attacking. However, we've never heard of a definite case of a woman losing an ear lobe this way, even though I see people swimming and diving with earrings all the time. The same goes for wedding bands. I keep mine on.

- **"The water in Hawai'i is too cold for comfort."**
  "The water is Hawai'i is as warm as bath water."

  It can be pretty cool, especially late winter, especially if you go in naked; but there is an alternative. Just wear a thin wetsuit and it will feel a lot like the Caribbean in summer. Or you can wait till late summer and give the water a chance to warm up. Don't expect warm water in Kaua'i in March.

- **"It rains all the time in Kaua'i."**
  "Kaua'i is too hot and sunny."
  "It's always windy in Kawa'i."

  In Kaua'i you can have the climate of your choice. Don't believe everything you read in advertising literature (like hotel brochures) regarding perfect weather. It does vary, there are seasons, and location matters. It just depends on your personal preferences. You may hit a patch of rain, but it seldom lasts for long. The typical weather report for Po'ipu is: Tonight – fair; Tomorrow, mostly sunny; for the weekend, sunny except for some upslope clouds in the afternoon. The drama of weather is part of the charm of the tropics – enjoy it as it is, rather than expecting it to be exactly as you want.

- **"Octopuses only come out at night."**

Some types are nocturnal, some not. We've seen lots in Hawai'i quite active during the day. The hard part is spotting them! Pay your dues, look sharp, and you'll see one eventually. The broad inner lagoon at 'Anini Beach is an excellent place to look.

- **"Kaua'i is getting too crowded and commercial."**

While there is certainly no problem buying a T-shirt in town or finding sun-worshippers on the beaches, there are plenty of spectacular sites to snorkel that are completely uncrowded. As long as you have a car, it's easy to drive to delightful and secluded locations – usually within half an hour from your hotel or condo. Hiking on Kaua'i can take you completely away from civilization as you know it, but a good map (such as ours) can lead you to some lovely snorkeling sites as well as romantic vistas to enjoy the sunset and the view of neighboring islands. And for really getting away from it all, try a trip to Lehua.

- **"The food is too expensive."**

Restaurant food is not inexpensive, but it also costs no more than in most major urban areas. In a grocery store, it does cost a fair amount more, especially fresh produce that must be flown in. But there are solutions. Rent a condo, pick up a trunk-load of staples at the market as you leave the airport, and check out the great variety of foods at the local grocery with Hawai'ian specialties. Try the hearty Hawai'ian "plate lunch", which is inexpensive and doesn't leave room for a full dinner. Be sure to check out the Kona coffee, local fresh fruits, Maui onions, and ever-popular bakeries and ice cream vendors. There's no reason to go hungry in Kaua'i.

Snorkeling the Internet

We figure some of you are really wired. Brought your laptop along to poolside just for fun? Just got one of those new SportsLaptops with the rubberized keyboard? Maybe you don't even have to get out of the water to log on the net, who knows?

We like speed, too, but book writing and publishing is still a slow business. You wouldn't believe how many long, hard hours we spend slaving away, snorkeling and researching, researching and snorkeling some more, in order to produce the little volume you're holding. Maybe a hundred hours of research gets distilled into one little page of maps and text. It makes me sweat just to think about it.

Oh, yeah, *some tough job*, I hear someone saying. We get no sympathy. But we have learned to live with that, and snorkel on. To enable the wired to get the latest corrections and additions between revisions, we've created **snorkelguides.com** We post links to Hawai'ian resources there, as well as updates to phone numbers, excursions, and many other goodies.

There are a lot of good resources on the Web, more every day. Check out our progress on other snorkeling guidebooks. Or you can find out how to order copies to send to all your friends. A great Christmas or birthday gift, a lot better than another pair of socks for good old Dad! Encourage healthy snorkeling!

We'd love to hear what you like or don't like about our books, and reports about your experiences snorkeling. If you've found a great snorkeling site anywhere in the world, let us know via e-mail if you can and we'll share some of our favorites, too. The Web is changing hourly, so the best way to get current links is to go to our Web page, and just click on them!

Warning: The Web is getting more and more commercial. It's a libertarian's dream, anarchic, free and open, unfettered and sometimes chaotic. The downside to this unregulated utopia: you can't tell whether someone has a hidden agenda, knows what they're talking about, or is just plain lying. Watch out! Remember to maintain a healthy skepticism as you surf the web. Many of the elaborate sites are commercial, so what seems to be an objective review might have been bought and paid for. Someone selling excursions may only list those that give them a big cut. Be streetwise as you enjoy the web, and you'll be OK.

Order Form

Snorkel Hawai'i books make great birthday or holiday gifts. Get that friend or loved one off their duff and off to Hawai'i to snorkel!

If you like Snorkel Kaua'i, and decide to give the other islands a try, we have some special deals available for repeat readers who buy more than one book at a time. Just make a photocopy of this order form, and mail it along with your check payable to:

> Indigo Publications
> 920 Los Robles Avenue
> Palo Alto, CA 94306
>
> one title: $14.00
>
> two titles: $25.00
>
> three titles: $34.00

Please order the following:

Quantity	Title
_____	Snorkel Hawai'i: The Big Island
_____	Snorkel Kaua'i
_____	Snorkel Maui and Lana'i
_____	price subtotal for books
_____	sales tax (CA residents only)
$ 2.00	shipping charge
_____	total enclosed

ship to: _____

_____

_____

Index

About the Authors

Judy and Mel Malinowski love to snorkel in the warm oceans of the tropics.

This love has led them to embark on snorkeling and cultural adventures to 60-some countries from Anguilla to Zanzibar. Hawai'i keeps drawing them back, and they are becoming kama'aina.

Although they are certified Scuba divers, the lightness and freedom of snorkeling keeps it their favorite recreation.

Mel, Judy and their three children have hosted students and cultural exchange visitors from Bosnia, Brazil, China, Germany, Nepal, New Zealand, Serbia, and Turkey in their home, and helped hundreds of other families enrich their lives through cultural exchange.

Working with exchange students and traveling as much as their businesses allow has encouraged their interest in the study of languages from Chinese to Spanish.

Graduates of Stanford University, they live in Santa Cruz,California.